Picture Credits
t=top b=bottom c=centre l=left r=right m=middle

Front Cover Images: Stephenmeese/Shutterstock, kristiansekulic/Shutterstock, Iouriitcheka/Shutterstock, Sergeypopovv/Shutterstock.

Back Cover Images: Rocksuzi/Dreamstime, Iouriitcheka/Shutterstock

Border Images: giangrandealessia/Shutterstock, bouzou/Shutterstock, Eliseishafer/Shutterstock, Morozovatatyana/Shutterstock, Specta/Shutterstock, coko/shutterstock

Insides: Serp/Shutterstock: 6t, Chris Gjersvik/Shutterstock: 6-7m, Ferenc Cegledi/shutterstock: 7t, Stephen Meese/Shutterstock: 8, cbpix/Shutterstock: 10, Phillipdate/Shutterstock: 11t, Jonald Morales/shutterstock: 12-13c, kristian sekulic/shutterstock: 13t, kristian sekulic/Shutterstock: 14, PBfo/Shutterstock: 15t, Wilc Both/Dreamstime: 15b, four oaks/ Shutterstock: 17ml, Davidmschrader/Dreamstime: 18t, XavierMarchant/Shutterstock: 18-19m, Yaniv Eliash/shutterstock: 20t, Musicstyleshoe/Dreamstime: 20b, DebraMcGuire/istock: 21, SashaDavas/Shutterstock: 22l, Dusanzidard/Shutterstock: 22-23m, Iourii Tcheka/Shutterstock: 24, Henrywilliam fu/Shutterstock: 25t, Henrywilliamfu/Shutterstock: 25b, Mhprice/Dreamstime: 26b, diarmuid/ Flickr: 27t, Pietervanpelt /istock: 27b, rpsycho/istock: 28-29t, Janmartin will/Shutterstock: 28b, Lazarevaevgeniya/istock: 29b, Sergeypopovv/Shutterestock: 30, Thomasbarrat/shutterstock: 31t, Dejanlazarevic/Shutterstock: 31b, Lenagrottling/shutterstock: 32, Taiga/shutterstock: 33t, Olga Bogatyrenko/Shutterstock: 33b, Romannikulenkov/Shutterstock; 35b, navy.mil: 36, Jamessteidl: 37b, michaelgatewood/ istock: 37t, Hiroshisato/Shutterstock: 38, Galinabarskaya/shutterstock: 39b, Markinterrante/ Flickr: 39t, Ximagination/Shutterstock: 40, Pavol Kmeto/Shutterstock: 41b, Jarnogonzalezzarraonandia/Shutterstock: 41t

Published By: North Parade Publishing Ltd.
4 North Parade, Bath, BA1 1LF, UK

First Published: 2008

Printed in China.

DISCOVER DOLPHINS

CONTENTS

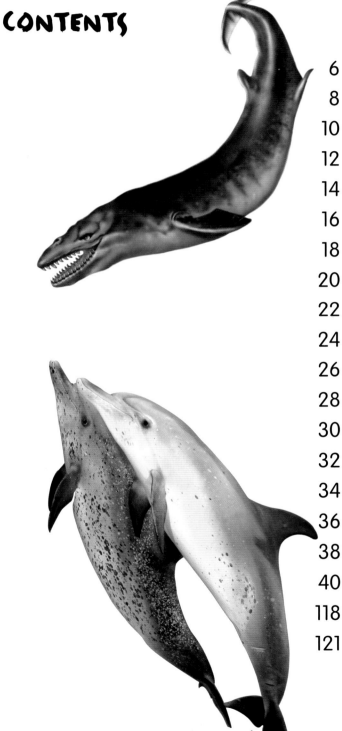

DISCOVER SHARKS

CONTENTS

DISCOVER WHALES

CONTENTS

DOLPHINS

Dolphins are some of the most fascinating creatures in the world. Their intelligence and friendliness make them endearing to humans.

 The open sea

WATERY HOMES

Dolphins are warm-blooded mammals that inhabit the aquatic world. They are found in almost every part of the world, with the Bottlenose dolphin being the most widely distributed. They usually prefer shallow waters around continental shelves and some dolphins, such as the Boto, are found in large river systems as well. Each species of dolphin are specially adapted to the area they live in, the food they eat, the predators they may face and the physical challenges they may encounter.

FUN FACT

The ancestors of the dolphins were actually land animals!

 There are many species of dolphin in the world and each of them has distinct characteristics and behavioural patterns

LOOK AT US

Dolphins are close cousins of whales and porpoises. They are, in fact, toothed whales belonging to the order Cetacea and the family Delphinidae. They are larger than porpoises and male dolphins are bigger than the females. Their teeth are conical, arranged around a beak-shaped mouth.

The distinct teeth and beak of a dolphin

WE ARE YOUNG!

Dolphin species evolved about ten million years ago during the Miocene period. Today there are as many as seventeen genera with around forty different species of dolphins in them. Different dolphin species vary in size, lying anywhere between 1.2–9.5 m (4–30 ft) in length, and 40 kg–10 tonnes (88 lbs–11.02 tons) in weight!

IN THE BEGINNING

Dolphins are relatively new to this world. They evolved in the Miocene period, around ten million years ago.

The dolphins' spine suggests they evolved from land animals

EARLY DOLPHINS

Dolphins evolved from mammals that once lived on land. They still retain certain land features. For example, all dolphins breathe in air, and some still have remnants of their hind legs. Also, the composition of their spines suggests that their ancestors ran on land and did not live in water.

FULLY AQUATIC

The early ancestors of the dolphin became fully aquatic around thirty-eight million years ago. The Basilosaurus and Dorudon were two such aquatic ancestors of dolphins. In fact, they looked very much like modern-day dolphins and whales, but they still had a long way to go before evolving into the highly intelligent animals we see today. They did not have the 'melon organ' that enables today's dolphins to make sounds. They also had smaller brains. This suggests that they liked to live alone and not socialise, unlike modern day dolphins.

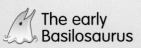 The early Basilosaurus

ON LAND

The early ancestors of dolphins were known as the Archaeoceti, or the ancient whales. These creatures probably evolved in the early Paleocene period, around 65 million years ago. They were completely land-based. It was only in the following period, the Eocene, that they started living in water more than on land. One such terrestrial ancestor of dolphins is known as the Pakicetus, which resembled the modern-day wolf.

Remains of the Pakicetus have been found in Pakistan

DOLPHIN SONGS

Dolphins are capable of producing different kinds of sounds. Some of these are used to communicate, while others are used to find their way and identify objects.

CLICKS AND WHISTLES

Dolphins can be very noisy animals. They make nasal sounds from airsacs below their blowholes. They make three main types of sounds: whistles, burst-pulse sounds and clicks. The first two are used to communicate with other dolphins. Clicks are used mainly to find their location, identify different objects and see how far they are from them. This is known as echolocation.

Dolphins open their mouths and produce three types of sounds: clicks, whistles and burst-pulses

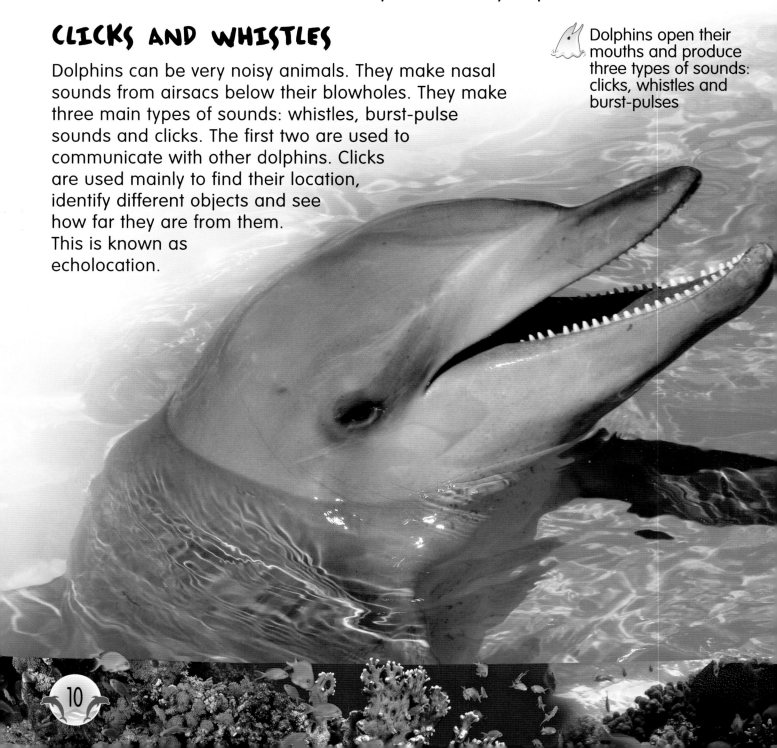

WHAT IS ECHOLOCATION?

Echolocation, also known as biosonar, is the ability to use echoes to locate objects. Many animals, such as bats, whales and dolphins, use this method. They emit sonar waves, which reflect off objects and bounce back to them as an echo. The time taken for the sound to travel from the animal to the object and back again, shows how far away the object is. Echolocation also helps to determine the size and location of other animals.

I CAN FIND MY WAY!

Dolphins produce high-frequency clicks from their nasal sacs located behind a melon-shaped organ in their head. These clicks are then narrowed into a thin beam by the melon and released into the environment, where they hit an object and come back as an echo, which is then received by the dolphin's lower jaw. From there it finally goes to the brain, helping them to find their way.

FUN FACT

Clicks emitted by dolphins for echolocation are among the loudest sounds made by any animal in the sea!

Bats also use echolocation to find their way

Sound-making Apparatus

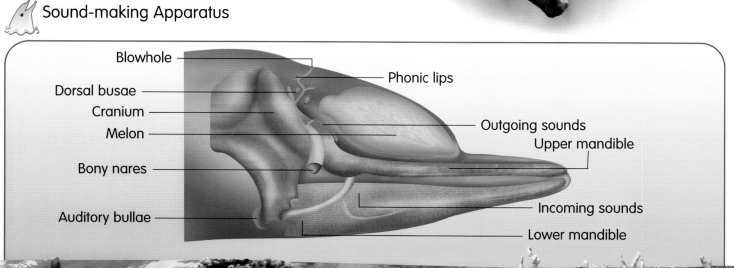

Blowhole

Dorsal busae

Cranium

Melon

Bony nares

Auditory bullae

Phonic lips

Outgoing sounds

Upper mandible

Incoming sounds

Lower mandible

MaKING SENSE

Dolphins use their excellent senses to make life easier underwater. These include hearing, sight and touch.

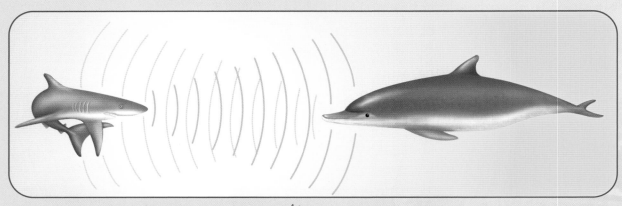

 Sound emitted by a dolphin is received by another in the lower jaw

I CAN HEAR YOU!

The dolphin's sense of hearing is very well developed. In fact, they can hear much better than humans. They have a small ear on each side of their head and their inner ears are covered by a bone called the auditory bulla. Sound enters through a fat-filled cavity in their lower jaw and travels to the middle ear. From there it is transferred to the brain. The middle ear has a large number of blood vessels, which balance pressure when they dive. A dolphin's ears also help in echolocation.

OTHER SENSES

Dolphins also have good eyesight, both under and above water, in bright as well as dim light. Some dolphins, such as the Bottlenose, have binocular vision above water. Their sense of touch is also highly developed. They are known to caress one another as a sign of affection. Although dolphins have almost no hair, they have some hair follicles, which help in their sense of touch.

NOT SO GOOD

The dolphin's sense of taste is not as acute as the other three senses. They do show a preference towards certain fish, but it is likely that this may have more to do with the texture of the fish rather than the taste. Dolphins do not have any sense of smell at all because they lack olfactory nerves.

Dolphins love to eat fish

Dolphins are very affectionate creatures

FUN FACT

Bottlenose dolphins can hear sounds within a frequency range of 1-150 kHz

SWIMMERS

Dolphins are perfectly adapted to their life underwater, from the shape and structure of their body, to what they eat and how they behave.

LIFE UNDERWATER

Dolphins have adapted to living underwater. They have sensitive skin on their lower jaws which allows them to identify small objects, and have a blowhole on top of their heads which enables them to breathe air from the surface. Their eyesight, both under and on the surface of water, is very well developed. With all these senses, life underwater is made easier.

Dolphins have blowholes on top of their heads, which help them to breathe air from the surface

SWIMMING CHAMPIONS

Most dolphins have streamlined bodies to help them move quickly underwater. and their skin secretes an oily substance which enables them to swim through water smoothly. Dolphins also have a complex system of nerves all over their bodies to make swimming more efficient. They have pectoral flippers and flukes, used mainly for steering underwater. Most species of dolphins have dorsal fins.

 Dorsal fins help dolphins to maintain their balance while swimming

MERGE WITH THE SURROUNDINGS

The form of camouflage seen in dolphins is known as countershade. Most dolphins are grey, grey-green or grey-brown on their backs. This fades to lighter grey and white on the underside. Viewed from above, they merge with the dark colours of the ocean. When seen from below they blend with the brighter colours of the ocean surface.

FUN FACT
Dolphins shed and re-grow their skin just like humans!

Countershade helps dolphins to blend with their surroundings and avoid predators

BRAINY CREATURES

Researchers all over the world are trying to understand dolphin intelligence. Some believe dolphins are more intelligent than dogs.

HOW BIG IS YOUR BRAIN?

The size of the brain of an animal in relation to its body is a very simple method of analysing intelligence. Big brains in proportion to bodies imply greater intelligence. Thi ratio in a dolphin is half of that of a human. But, if we exclude the weight of the fatty blubber, then this ratio is much closer. However, it is difficult to compare the brain functions of a water-dwelling animal with that of a land animal because they are designed to perform completely different kinds of tasks.

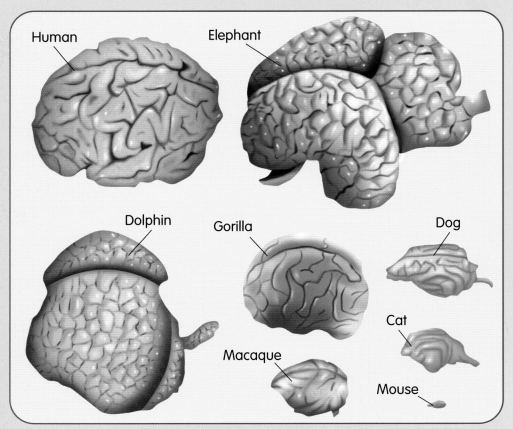

Human
Elephant
Dolphin
Gorilla
Dog
Macaque
Cat
Mouse

 Size of brain in relation to the body is one way to measure intelligence

FUN FACT

Newborn Bottlenose dolphins have 42% of the brain mass of an adult dolphin. With humans this figure is only 25%.

MIRROR REFLECTION

Researchers have tried to study whether dolphins are self-aware. Self-awareness means whether they can look at their mirror reflections and understand what they are seeing, thus indicating a highly developed level of intelligence. In this respect, different species of dolphins show different degrees of self-awareness and experiments have proved that Bottlenose dolphins are self-aware.

The ability to recognise oneself in the mirror is called self-awareness

Dolphins may be as intelligent as elephants

PROBLEMS AND SOLUTIONS

The ability to solve simple and complex problems is seen as a clear sign of intelligence. Dolphins perform very well when tested for their problem-solving ability. Also they have also shown abstract abilities, such as telling the difference between numbers. Some scientists believe that dolphins are as intelligent as elephants.

WE ARE FAMILY

Dolphins are known to have strong familial bonds.
They live together in groups, known as pods.

 Thousands of dolphins join to form superpods. These dolphins can be seen travelling together

GROUPING TOGETHER

Dolphins are social animals and live in groups called pods. Sometimes, many groups join together and form a superpod comprising thousands of dolphins. Pods join together when they are under threat, are frightened, or because of familial associations. Dolphins in a pod tend to form strong bonds with one another and are known to help other dolphins in trouble. Within the pod, an hierarchy is formed amongst the male dolphins, displayed through behaviour such as tail slapping.

HELLO THERE!

Dolphins make unique whistle sounds, known as signature whistles, to either call another dolphin or identify themselves. Each dolphin's unique signature whistle is developed early in life and closely resembles the whistle of their mothers. Another type of sound they make is called a burst-pulse sound. These appear to depend upon their emotional state, for example, they may squawk or bark when angry and squeak when being playful. These sounds travel into the ultrasound range.

 Humans have recorded the inaudible sounds made by dolphins

CREATIVE ANIMALS

Dolphins are capable of learning complex routines when there is reward waiting for them. Studies into dolphin learning were carried out by a scientist named Karen Pryor in the 1960s. She used two dolphins and rewarded them with food in order to encourage them when they exhibited the desired behaviour. Over time she was able to teach the dolphins a series of complex routines.

Dolphins can be creative. This is seen in the various ways in which they move

MAMA MIA!

Like many living creatures, dolphins protect and take care of their young.

A LONG WAIT

Most dolphins carry their babies for a gestation period of 12–17 months. At the end of this, they give birth to one calf. Although dolphins are capable of giving birth every two years, they usually have intervals of three years. They are known to help one another during the birth of the calves, and help take care of them afterwards.

 Dolphin calves stay close to their mothers. They are often seen swimming next to their mothers, even in large pods

Dolphin calves are encouraged to the surface as soon as they are born, so that they can breathe

MY MOTHER TOLD ME

Dolphins can learn how to use simple tools. Some will use a natural sponge to protect their nose while hunting. This knowledge is passed down by mothers to the young. Female dolphins stay with their pods, but male dolphins often leave and form groups of their own. The signature whistles of individual dolphins are developed during childhood.

BABY DOLPHINS

A newborn dolphin calf is about 1 m (3 ft) long and 16 kg (35 lbs) in weight. In the days shortly after their birth, they have soft and weak tail flukes and dorsal fins which gradually harden over time. Mother dolphins start nursing their calves around six hours after giving birth and may continue for up to 18 months. Calves stay with their mothers for a maximum of six years, during which time they learn how to hunt for food, live in social groups and interact with other dolphins.

Dolphin calves are darker in colour than adult dolphins

DO I SMELL FOOD?

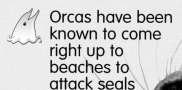 Orcas have been known to come right up to beaches to attack seals

Dolphins use different methods of feeding, and their diet consists of fish and squid.

FEEDING METHODS

Herding is one clever method of catching food employed by dolphins. Here, a pod of dolphins work together to group a school of fish while individual members take turns to feed. Another common method is known as corralling, where fish are chased until they reach shallow waters and are easily captured. Some dolphins, such as the Atlantic Bottlenose, use the strand feeding method. Here, the fish are chased onto mud banks and then can be easily scooped up.

FUN FACT

Adult Bottlenose dolphins eat as much as 4-5 per cent of their body weight daily.

WHERE'S THE WATER!

Despite having water all around them, dolphins don't drink seawater because it is too salty. Instead, dolphins acquire the water they need from the food that they eat. Moreover, when fat is burnt in their bodies, it releases more water.

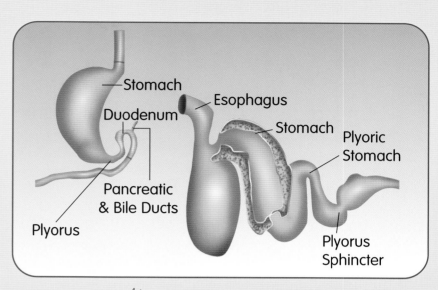

Labels: Stomach, Esophagus, Duodenum, Stomach, Plyoric Stomach, Pancreatic & Bile Ducts, Plyorus, Plyorus Sphincter

Dolphins have a special digestive system, which releases large quantities of water from their food

SOMETHING SMELLS GOOD!

A dolphin's diet usually consists of fish, squid and shrimp. The quantity of food they eat depends on the size of their prey. For big fish, such as herring or mackerel, the quantity can be much less than for squid or shrimp. Their stomachs have different compartments to aid digestion. They also have a very strong muscle in their throat, which allows them to swallow their food without taking in seawater.

Dolphins like to eat fish, such as herring, cod, sardines and mackerel

SEA ACROBATS

Leaping and jumping out of water is a common sight among dolphins. These playful creatures are known to be very acrobatic.

PLAY TIME

Dolphins are very playful, intelligent creatures, and are often seen jumping out of the water and performing acrobatics. This behaviour is known as breaching. Dolphins can also be seen riding on waves created by boats or ships. This has probably developed from their natural habit of riding on swells created by whales or swimming alongside their mothers as calves. They are often seen playing, tossing seaweed, carrying objects, mock fighting and chasing one another. They chase other creatures as well, such as turtles or sea birds, for fun.

FUN FACT

A dolphin can jump as high as 4.9 m (16.1 ft) from the water.

 Dolphins love to play and are often seen chasing each other

WHAT DO WE KNOW?

Scientists around the world are fascinated by the dolphin's breaching behaviour. Some believe that dolphins jump out of water to view prey from above and to look for signs, such as feeding birds, to help locate prey. The behaviour may also be a form of communication, a sign to other dolphins to join the hunt, and showing which direction they're heading. Dislodging parasites is another possible reason for breaching; or perhaps dolphins leap and jump and spin simply for fun!

 Jumping high into the air and then falling on their backs or sides is known as breaching

SPINNING AROUND

Some of the most interesting acrobatic moves are performed by Spinner dolphins. They can jump out of the water and barrel roll. These are small, usually dark grey dolphins, with long and thin beaks. It is not certain as to why these dolphins spin but one explanation is that the bubbles created during spinning helps with echolocation.

Spinner dolphins will often perform several barrel rolls in succession

DOLPHIN FAMILY

The Delphinidae is the largest family among all the Cetacea, and includes many species with different sizes, shapes and characteristics.

WE ARE NOT COMMON

There are two types of Common dolphin – the Long-beaked and the Short-beaked, distinguished by the length of their beaks. Some scientists have also identified a third type of Common dolphin, which have extremely long, thin beaks. Common dolphins can be found all over the world, in tropical, sub-tropical and temperate waters, particularly in the Mediterranean and Red seas. They travel in large active pods of 100–2000 dolphins.

Common dolphins usually travel in groups of 10–50

FUN FACT

There are as many as 67 species in the Delphinidae family.

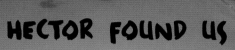

HECTOR FOUND US

Hector's dolphins are some of the smallest Cetacean in the world. An adult is usually 1.2-1.6 m (4-5.25 ft) in length, and weighs about 50 kg (110 lbs). These dolphins are named after Sir James Hector, curator of the Colonial Museum in Wellington, who first studied them. Hector's dolphins do not have pronounced beaks like many other species. They have a grey forehead, white throat and chest and a dark shade of grey running from their eyes to their flippers.

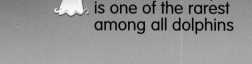

The Hector's dolphin is one of the rarest among all dolphins

WE ARE DUSKY

Dusky dolphins are very active and friendly. They are usually found around coastal regions in the Southern Hemisphere and the largest ones have been found off the coast of Peru. They can be as long as 210 cm (82.7 in) and weigh about 100 kg (220.5 lbs). The main danger facing these friendly dolphins is being trapped in fishing nets.

Dusky dolphins can cover vast distances. But such movements may have nothing to do with their migration

NO KILLER

Killer Whales are actually dolphins and the largest among all ocean-living dolphins. They are found in all the oceans of the world, from extremely warm to extremely cold regions.

BLACK AND WHITE

Killer Whales are easily distinguishable because of their black backs, white chests and sides and white patch near their eyes. They have large, heavy bodies, the largest weighing over 8 tonnes (17,636 lbs) and measuring about 9.8 m (32 ft) in length. It is this bulk that gives them the strength to move very fast. They have been known to move at speeds of 56 km/h (35 mph). Male Killer Whales are usually larger than females. One feature that helps to distinguish individual Killer Whales, is the pattern of white or grey saddle patches on their dorsal fins. Killer Whales are also known as Orcas.

I'M ON A DIET

Killer Whales are opportunistic hunters. Their diet consists mostly of fish, particularly salmon, herring and tuna. Some Killer Whales are also known to hunt sea lions, seals, whales, and even sharks. It is common for them to disable their prey first before killing and eating them. Killer Whales are sometimes called Seawolves because they hunt in packs, much like wolves on land.

 Birds such as penguins and seagulls can also fall prey to Orcas

SOCIAL ANIMALS

Killer Whales are known to be social animals. This can be seen through behaviour such as spyhopping, tail slapping and breaching. Some of them have very complex social groupings. Killer Whales have matrilineal societies, which means there is a single dominant mother and both her male and female young live with her for the whole of their lives. When a few of such matrilineal groups join together, they form a pod. But these pods are not as stable as the individual groups. A group of pods joining together is known as a clan and a group of clans joining together is known as a community.

Killer Whales can be easily spotted because of their black and white bodies

FUN FACT

Different groups of Killer Whales have sets of calls that are specific to them. These are known as dialects.

Killer Whales have complex social structures and live in large pods

HUMAN FRIENDS

Throughout the ages the interaction between dolphins and humans has been friendly and special.

WILL YOU PLAY WITH ME?

Dolphins and humans have always been known to share a friendly and playful relationship. Many species of dolphins, particularly the Bottlenose, adapt well to human company. They can also be trained to perform clever tricks and important tasks. They are studied with great interest by scientists all over the world. The level of intelligence among dolphins is a subject that has long fascinated us.

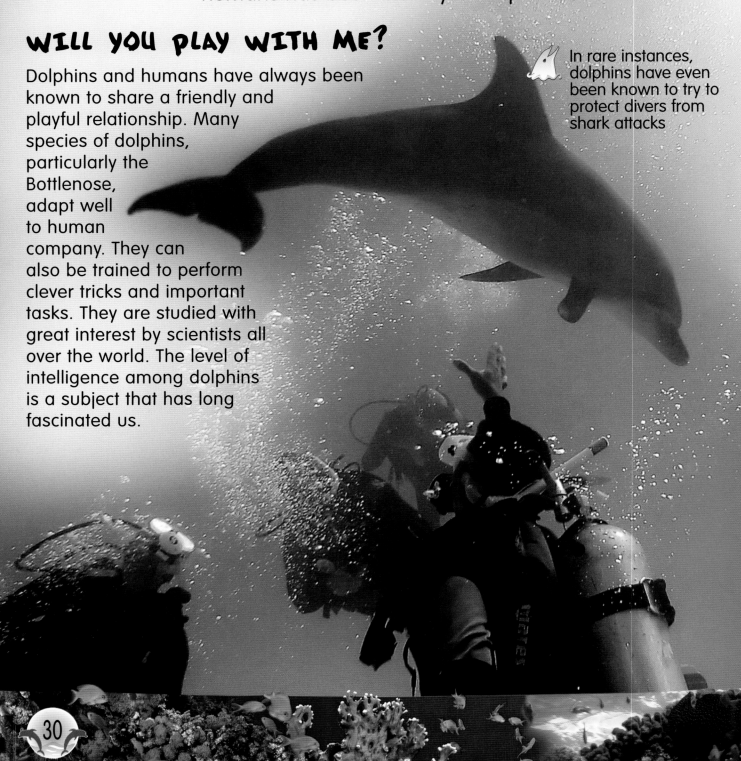

In rare instances, dolphins have even been known to try to protect divers from shark attacks

THEY ARE EVERYWHERE

Dolphins feature in the human world in various fields. They are used in the military, in entertainment and in therapy. References to dolphins are also widespread in mythology, as well as literature, art, popular movies and even television series.

Dolphins are even used in therapy

IN THE WILD

It is clear that humans are fascinated by dolphins, but do dolphins enjoy human company as much? Possibly not! Harmful human activities, such as contamination and pollution of seas and oceans with dangerous toxins, have destroyed dolphin habitats and killed many dolphins. Moreover, it must always be kept in mind that dolphins are animals of the wild. So, it is more natural that they would want to avoid human company rather than seek it.

Pollution affects dolphin habitats and ecosystems

ENTERTAINERS

Dolphins feature prominently in different forms of entertainment, such as aqariums, movies and even computer games.

Dolphins are known for their performing abilities

DOLPHIN AQUARIUMS

Dolphins are among the most popular performing animals. People flock to aquariums, where dolphins perform impressive and complicated routines. The most common species of dolphins used for performance are Bottlenose because they live long, look friendly and are easy to train. Some people argue that it is cruel to make dolphins perform for our pleasure. However, there are now strict guidelines as to the welfare of dolphins in captivity.

FUN FACT

In the early part of the 1970s around 37 dolphin aquariums and travelling shows existed in the UK.
Today there are none.

NOT SO SAFE

Dolphin aquariums have been criticised by many on several grounds. Critics say that dolphins in captivity do not have enough space to move about freely, even if the pools are very large. They have also been known to become aggressive and can attack each other, their trainers or even audience participants. Hence, strict rules regulating animal welfare have been imposed, which has led to the closure of many dolphin aquariums around the world.

 Dolphin aquariums have often been criticised by activists

The Miami Dolphins use a dolphin as their mascot and logo

MOVIE STARS

Dolphins have been widely popularised by well-known movies and television series, including *Flipper, Free Willy* and *The Day of the Dolphin* on the big screen, and *Flipper* and *SeaQuest DSV* on television.

MYTHOLOGY & LITERATURE

Dolphins have long captivated the imaginations of humans. They are a popular theme in mythology, literature and art.

IN ANCIENT GREECE

Greek mythology is full of references to dolphins. Many Greek gods and heroes were rescued by dolphins, including the poet, Arion, the God, Melicertes and the legendary character, Phalanthus. They were also believed to be the Greek sea God, Poseidon's, messenger. They were sacred to the Greeks.

A dolphin is said to have saved the poet Arion

FUN FACT

Dolphin myths help us to understand where they were once found.

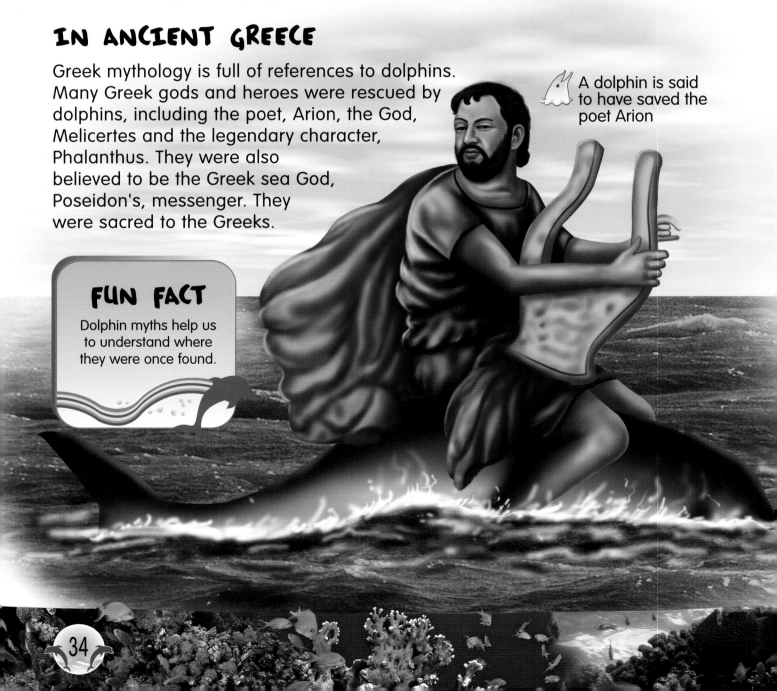

OTHER MYTHOLOGY

In Hindu mythology, the goddess Ganga was closely associated with Ganges River dolphins. One such myth tells the story of how the dolphin was one of the creatures that heralded the Goddess' coming down from heaven. The dolphin is sometimes shown as the Goddess' mount, called Makara. In the regions around the Amazon River a popular myth is that the Boto, a river dolphin, can change into a handsome young man!

Pots and vases decorated with dolphin images were popular among the Greeks

The goddess Ganga's mount, the dolphin named Makara is sacred to the Hindus

LITERATURE & ART

Dolphins are particularly popular in science fiction novels, including Anne McCaffrey's *The Dragonriders of Pern* series and a short story by William Gibson called *Johnny Mnemonic*. *The Music of Dolphins*, by Karen Hesse, is a moving story about a dolphin-human relationship. Dolphins are also popular in art. The Greeks were known to paint dolphins on vases.

MILITARY & THERAPY

Dolphins are intelligent and very trainable creatures,
which is why they are used to serve diverse human purposes.

MILITARY DOLPHINS

Military
dolphins
are trained
from a very
young age

Dolphins used for military purposes are known as military dolphins. They are trained to perform tasks, such as locating mines underwater and rescuing lost divers. The training of dolphins for military use was first started during the Cold War by the USA and former Soviet Union. The US military still runs an open program for the training of military dolphins, known as the US Navy Marine Mammal Program. They were used by the US military during the first Gulf War and also in the recent Iraq War. The Russian military reportedly closed down their marine mammal program during the 1990s.

DOLPHIN PSYCHIATRISTS

Dolphins are sometimes used for the psychiatric treatment of people suffering from depression and for aiding in therapy of autistic and brain damaged individuals. Such programmes are known as Dolphin Assisted Therapy, or DAT.

In 2005, a study involving around 30 people suffering from mild to moderate depression, revealed that contact with dolphins had a positive effect on their mood.

 A child enjoys being in the water with a dolphin

DANGEROUS TASKS

The practise of training dolphins for military use has been condemned by many all over the world. It is argued that dolphins come under a lot of stress in captivity. This leads to aggressive behaviour, shortening of lifespan and greater instances of infant mortality. Moreover, introducing them to war zones can be very harmful for these creatures, both physically and mentally.

FUN FACT

The theory behind Dolphin Assisted Therapy was given a new life by Dr. John Lilly during the 1950s and 60s.

War zones can be dangerous for dolphins

HYBRIDS

Some animals are born of parents belonging to different species. These are known as hybrids.

WHOLPHINS

Wholphins are a hybrid of the False Killer Whale and Bottlenose dolphin. Only two exist in captivity. At the moment they can both be found at the Sea Life Park in Hawaii. They are a mother-daughter pair.

FUN FACT

Many hybrids are infertile. That is, they cannot reproduce.

Kekaimalu's daughter, Kawili'Kai was fathered by a Bottlenose dolphin

MOTHER AND DAUGHTERS

The famous captive Wholphin, Kekaimalu, housed at the Sea Life Park in Hawaii, gave birth to a calf at a very young age, which did not survive long. She gave birth to a second calf in 1991, that passed away when it was 9 years old. The Wholphin then gave birth to a third calf named Kawili'Kai, in December 2004. This time she was able to nurse the calf and it survived to adulthood.

Wholphins are very rare in the wild. Only two exist in captivity

IN NATURE & IN CAPTIVITY

Hybrids between different species of dolphin have been found in nature as well, such as the Bottlenose-Atlantic Spotted dolphin and Wholphin. Very few have ever been spotted in the wild, although some may be found in the waters of Hawaii.

THREATS AND DANGERS

The greatest threat faced by dolphins is not from nature but from the cruel hunting methods and harmful activities of humans.

NATURAL THREATS

In nature, dolphins hardly have any enemies at all. This makes them apex predators, or top predators, in their particular habitat. Only some large species of sharks, such as Great White sharks, Dusky sharks, Bull sharks and Tiger sharks, prey on smaller dolphins, particularly calves. Also, larger dolphins, like Orcas, sometimes prey on smaller dolphins. But instances of this are infrequent. Another threat to dolphins from nature are parasites, which cause diseases. Dolphins are usually strong and intelligent enough to overcome most challenges offered by nature.

FUN FACT

A survey conducted in 2006 revealed that there are no Yangtze River dolphins left anymore, which means that the species is now functionally extinct.

Great White sharks hunt small dolphins and are one of its few natural predators

DRIVEN TO THEIR DEATH

In some parts of the world dolphins are hunted for their meat. One method of hunting is known as dolphin drive hunting. Using this method, dolphins and other smaller Cetacean are herded together by boats and then driven onto the beach. Here, they are defenceless and can be killed easily by the hunters.

HUMAN MENACE

The greatest threat to the survival of dolphins comes from humans. Harmful and dangerous practises, such as dumping waste into rivers, seas and oceans, leads to the poisoning of dolphin habitats. Some dolphins perish as a result of accidents with propeller boats. One of the greatest threats comes from certain fishing methods, where dolphins become entangled in the nets and drown. Much of the world has banned these nets, but, tragically, there are still some countries that use them.

 Dolphins can even be affected by line fishing

A Shark's Tale

Sharks are amongst the most feared creatures on Earth, and only the very brave dare to go near them. They are meat lovers and have been around since before even the dinosaurs! Found in oceans, seas and rivers, they rule the waters with their sharp teeth and swift movements. Sharks are related to fish, yet they differ in many ways.

Dorsal fin

Bony matters

While most fish have skeletons made of bones, the shark skeleton is made up entirely of cartilage. Cartilage is the same flexible material that is found inside your ears and nose. It makes the shark lighter in weight and helps it to swim faster.

Long pointed snout

First dorsal fin

Second dorsal fin

Symmetrical Caudal fin

Gill slits

Pectoral fin

Barbel

Pectoral fin

Most fish have bony skeletons

Living dens

Sharks can be found in most oceans and seas. Large and more active sharks usually stay near the surface or the middle of the ocean. The smaller ones prefer the ocean floor. Some sharks live near the coast and can even enter rivers and lakes that are linked to the sea.

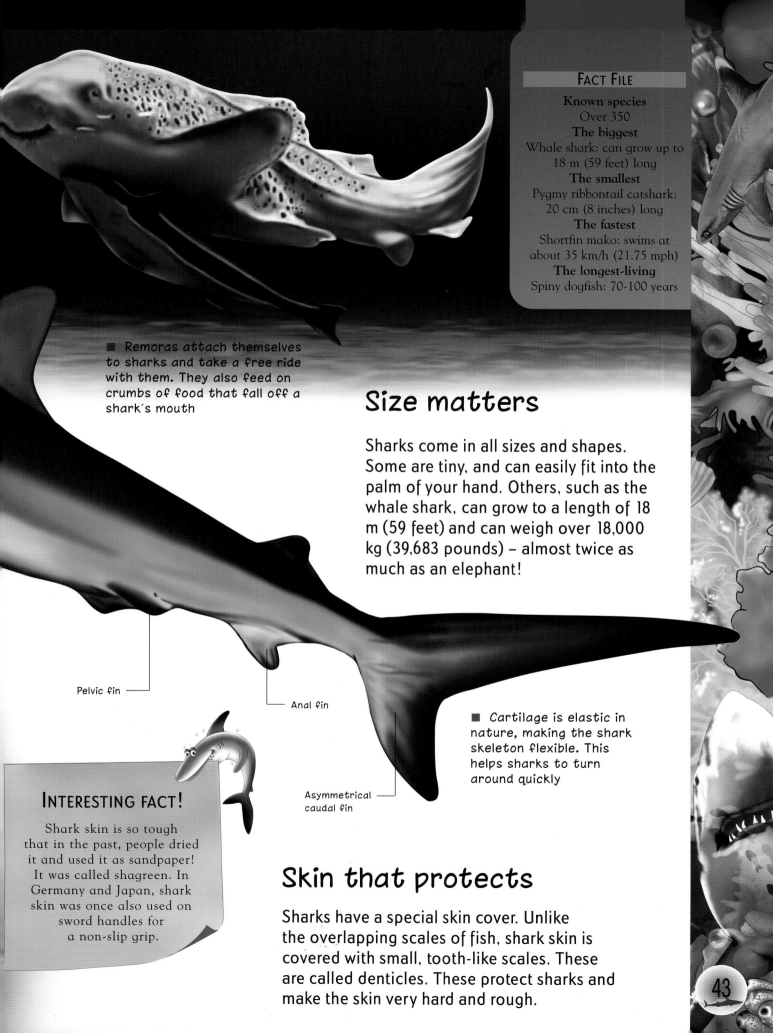

FACT FILE

Known species
Over 350
The biggest
Whale shark: can grow up to
18 m (59 feet) long
The smallest
Pygmy ribbontail catshark:
20 cm (8 inches) long
The fastest
Shortfin mako: swims at
about 35 km/h (21.75 mph)
The longest-living
Spiny dogfish: 70-100 years

■ Remoras attach themselves to sharks and take a free ride with them. They also feed on crumbs of food that fall off a shark's mouth

Size matters

Sharks come in all sizes and shapes. Some are tiny, and can easily fit into the palm of your hand. Others, such as the whale shark, can grow to a length of 18 m (59 feet) and can weigh over 18,000 kg (39,683 pounds) – almost twice as much as an elephant!

Pelvic fin

Anal fin

■ Cartilage is elastic in nature, making the shark skeleton flexible. This helps sharks to turn around quickly

Asymmetrical caudal fin

INTERESTING FACT!

Shark skin is so tough that in the past, people dried it and used it as sandpaper! It was called shagreen. In Germany and Japan, shark skin was once also used on sword handles for a non-slip grip.

Skin that protects

Sharks have a special skin cover. Unlike the overlapping scales of fish, shark skin is covered with small, tooth-like scales. These are called denticles. These protect sharks and make the skin very hard and rough.

43

In the Beginning...

Most creatures go through evolution, or change their features to adapt to their environment. But sharks are good survivors and have had little need to change in the last 150 million years.

Few fossils

Fossils are the dead remains of animals that stay preserved for hundreds of millions of years. Fossils have helped us study evolution. But a shark's skeleton crumbles quickly, as it is made of cartilage. Complete shark fossils, therefore, have not been found. All the fossils that have been found have been limited to their teeth and spines from their fins.

■ The Helicoprions lived 250 million years ago. Their jaws had a spiral-tooth setting, with smaller teeth on the front and larger ones at the back

Earliest sharks

Scientists believe that the ancestors of modern-day sharks appeared 350 to 400 million years ago, a time known as the Age of Fish, or the Devonian Period. This was 100 million years before dinosaurs existed. The earliest shark fossils are found in Antarctica and Australia.

INTERESTING FACT!

It is believed that extinct sharks had short, round snouts, while most modern sharks have long and pointed snouts. Some even have saw-like snouts.

■ The Orthacanthus lived in fresh waters and had V-shaped teeth. This species is now extinct

MEGALODON
Tooth size
Around 15 cm
(6 inches) long
Was found around
Europe, India,
Australia, America
Weighed
Over 35 tons (77,162
pounds), equal to the weight
of 12 elephants
Length
More than 16 m (52.5 feet)
Jaws opened up
1.8 m (6 feet) wide and
2.1 m (7 feet) high

■ A Megalodon tooth

■ A full-grown
human, standing
at 1.8 m (6 feet),
would have been
just as big as the
Megalodon's fin

The mega monster

One extinct shark known for its huge fossil teeth is the Megalodon.
It lived between 25 and 1.6 million years ago. Each of the
Megalodon's teeth was the size of a full-grown person's hand!
Scientists believe it was probably longer than 16 m (52.5 feet). It may
have been similar in appearance to the great white shark and is
thought to have fed on whale meat.

Modern sharks

Most modern-day sharks stopped evolving a long time ago. They have changed
very little in the last 100 million years. But scientists are still not sure about how
many kinds of sharks exist today. They continue to discover new species.

Body Basics

Living in the water can be tough. To meet this challenge, sharks are equipped with special features. All sharks have strong jaws, a pair of fins and nostrils and a flexible skeleton. Sharks are great swimmers but, unlike fish, they cannot move backwards.

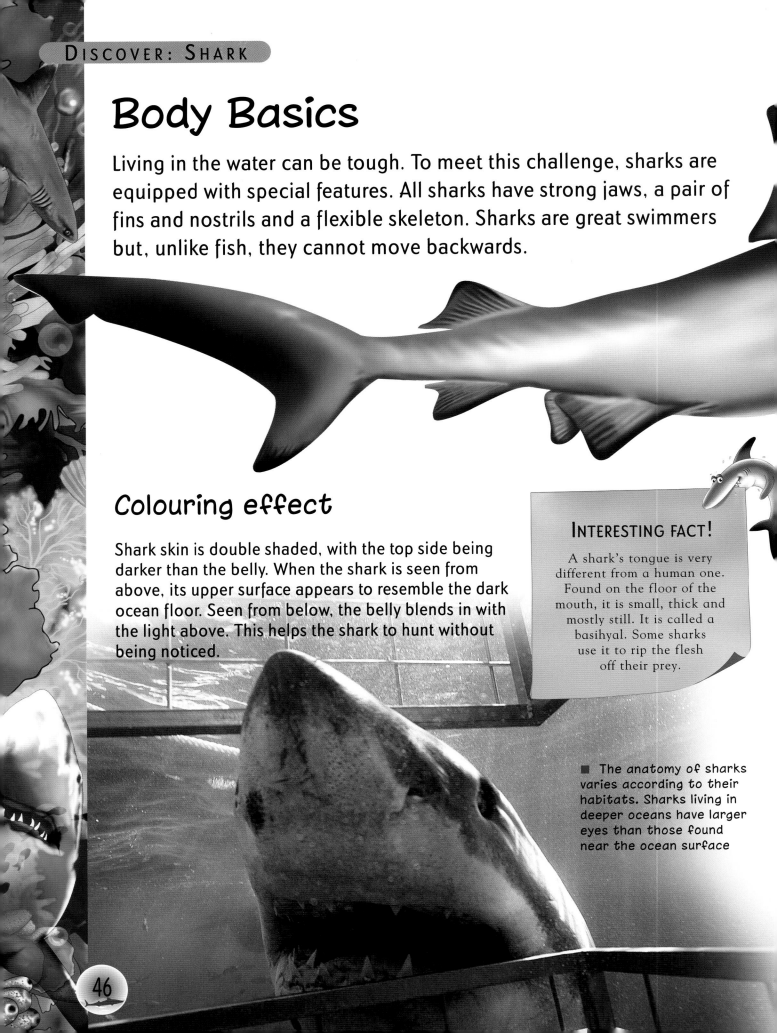

Colouring effect

Shark skin is double shaded, with the top side being darker than the belly. When the shark is seen from above, its upper surface appears to resemble the dark ocean floor. Seen from below, the belly blends in with the light above. This helps the shark to hunt without being noticed.

INTERESTING FACT!

A shark's tongue is very different from a human one. Found on the floor of the mouth, it is small, thick and mostly still. It is called a basihyal. Some sharks use it to rip the flesh off their prey.

■ The anatomy of sharks varies according to their habitats. Sharks living in deeper oceans have larger eyes than those found near the ocean surface

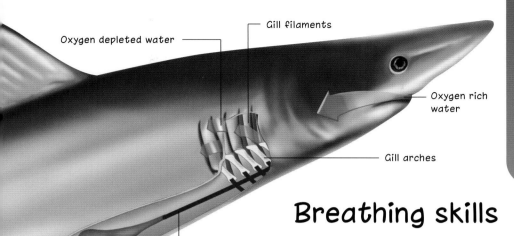

■ Unlike the gills of bony fish, shark gills do not have covers. Water must continue to flow across the gill slits for the shark to breathe

Oxygen depleted water

Gill filaments

Oxygen rich water

Gill arches

Heart

Ventral aorta

Breathing skills

Sharks, like fish, take oxygen from water. They have gill slits on either side of their heads. Water enters these slits and passes over the gill chambers, where oxygen is absorbed. Some sharks need to swim continuously to breathe, while others open and close their mouths to pump the water in.

■ Most sharks have five pairs of gills, while bony fish have just one. The broadnose sevengill shark, however, has seven pairs of gills

Oil Tank!

The largest organ in a shark is the liver, which is filled with oil. Since oil is lighter than water, it keeps the shark from sinking. Despite this, sharks must swim constantly to keep afloat. The liver also functions as a storehouse of energy.

Torpedo-like!

Most sharks have a rounded body that tapers at both ends. This torpedo-like shape helps them while swimming. But some sharks, like the angelshark, have a flat body. This helps them to live at the bottom of the ocean.

■ Sharks usually have blunt snouts. But sawsharks have long snouts with toothed edges, which help them to dig out prey from the ocean floor or to slash at fish passing by

■ The unique shape of the hammerhead shark's head helps it to get a better view of its surroundings

Shark Senses

Sharks have all the senses that humans do – and something extra too! Sharks can not only smell, see, feel, hear and taste. They also have a sixth sense. Their senses help them to hunt and travel great distances.

Surface Pore

Canal

Main Tube

Sensory cells

■ Lateral line canals are lined by tiny hair-like structures. Any movement in the water hits these hair-like structures, causing them to send a message to he brain

Line of action

Sharks have fluid-filled canals that run from head to toe on both sides of their body. This is called the lateral line. It enables the shark to sense movements in water. Some scientists believe that the lateral line can also detect low sounds.

Sixth sense

While electricity usually comes from wires and batteries, all living creatures also produce weak electric fields. Sharks are able to detect these with the help of their sixth sense. Tiny pores on the shark's snout lead to jelly-filled sacs known as the ampullae of Lorenzini that help them detect electrical fields

Lateral line canals

Smelly matters

In general, the nostrils of sharks are located on the underside of their snouts. They are used for smelling and not for breathing. Some sharks have nasal barbels, which look like thick whiskers sticking out from the bottom of the snout. Barbels help the shark to feel and taste.

■ Blind sharks cannot see. They hunt for their prey by using their nasal barbels

FACT FILE

In clear water, shark eyes
can see up to a distance
of 15 m (50 feet)
They hear sounds in the
frequency of 25 to 100 Hz
Can smell blood
400 m (1,312 feet) away
Sharks hear from as far as
250 m (820 feet)
Their taste buds
are in the mouth, and not
on the tongue

■ Certain sharks, such as the nurse
shark, have openings called spiracles
just behind their eyes. The shark
uses these spiracles to breathe
while hunting or feeding

Looking on

Sharks have very good eyesight, even better than
ours. A shark's eye, like that of a cat, can contract
or expand according to the light. This helps them
to see in dim light. Sharks can also see colours.

INTERESTING FACT!

Sharks do not have
external ear flaps. Instead,
their ears are inside their
heads, on both sides of the
brain case. Each ear leads
to a small pore on the
shark's head.

■ The great white shark has
a keen sense of smell. It can
detect a drop of blood in
100 litres (176 pints) of water!

Toothy Terrors

A shark's only proper weapon is its mouth. The mouth is below the snout in all species except the angelshark, the megamouth, whale shark and wobbegong shark. These species have their mouths at the end of their snouts. The two most important parts of a shark's mouth are the teeth and the jaws.

Tearing and crushing

Sharks do not chew their food, but gulp it down whole. They use their teeth only to tear the food into mouth-sized pieces. Some sharks also crush the shell of their prey with their teeth.

Big bite

In most animals, the lower jaw moves freely, but the upper jaw is attached to the skull. However, in sharks, the upper jaw rests below the skull. It moves out when the shark attacks its prey. This allows the shark to push its entire mouth forward to grab its victim. As the lower jaw teeth puncture and hold the prey, the upper jaw teeth slice it.

Great white shark

Mako

Sand tiger

■ Different types of shark teeth

■ The great white has large wedge-shaped teeth with jagged edges. The teeth of the Megalodon were three times larger than those of the great white

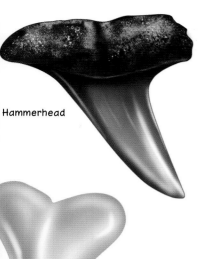

Hammerhead

Blue shark

Sharp new ones

Shark teeth fall out all the time. This is crucial, as worn out or broken teeth are continually replaced by new and sharper ones. The process takes place as often as every two weeks. In some sharks, like the great white, these teeth are arranged in several rows.

Tooth types

Sharks have a variety of teeth. Some have molar-like teeth, which help in the process of grinding. Others have razor-like cutting or pointed teeth.

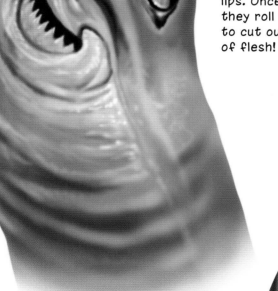

■ Cookie-cutter sharks eat their prey by attaching themselves to it with special sucking lips. Once attached, they roll their body to cut out a chunk of flesh!

INTERESTING FACT!

The basking shark has very tiny teeth. It does not use them to feed. Instead, the shark swallows plankton-rich water. Special bristles inside its mouth, called gill rakers, filter this food as the water flows through them.

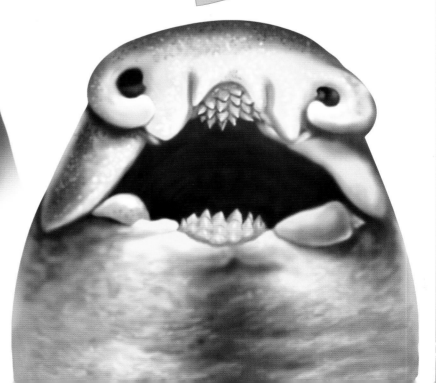

■ The Port Jackson shark does not have jagged teeth. Its front teeth are pointed for grasping its prey, while the back teeth are flat and molar-like for crushing

Young Ones

Baby sharks are called pups. A single litter could contain more than 100 pups! There are three different ways in which shark pups are born.

Laying eggs

Some sharks lay eggs like birds. The mother deposits the egg cases in the sea. The baby inside the egg gets its food from the yolk until the egg hatches. The parents do not protect the eggs. Horn sharks and swell sharks are egg-laying sharks. Such sharks are known as oviparous sharks.

Birth of a shark

Sharks like the hammerhead give birth to pups. The eggs hatch inside the mother's body and the babies get their food from the mother directly. Sharks that give birth to their young in this manner are called viviparous sharks. Lemon sharks, hammerheads, bull sharks and whale sharks are all types of viviparous sharks.

■ Horn shark eggs are spiral shaped and hatch six to nine months after being laid. The pups are usually 15-17 cm (5.9-6.7 inches) long

■ Certain shark's eggs are also called mermaid's purses because of their pouch-like appearance. The egg contains yolk that the baby feeds on

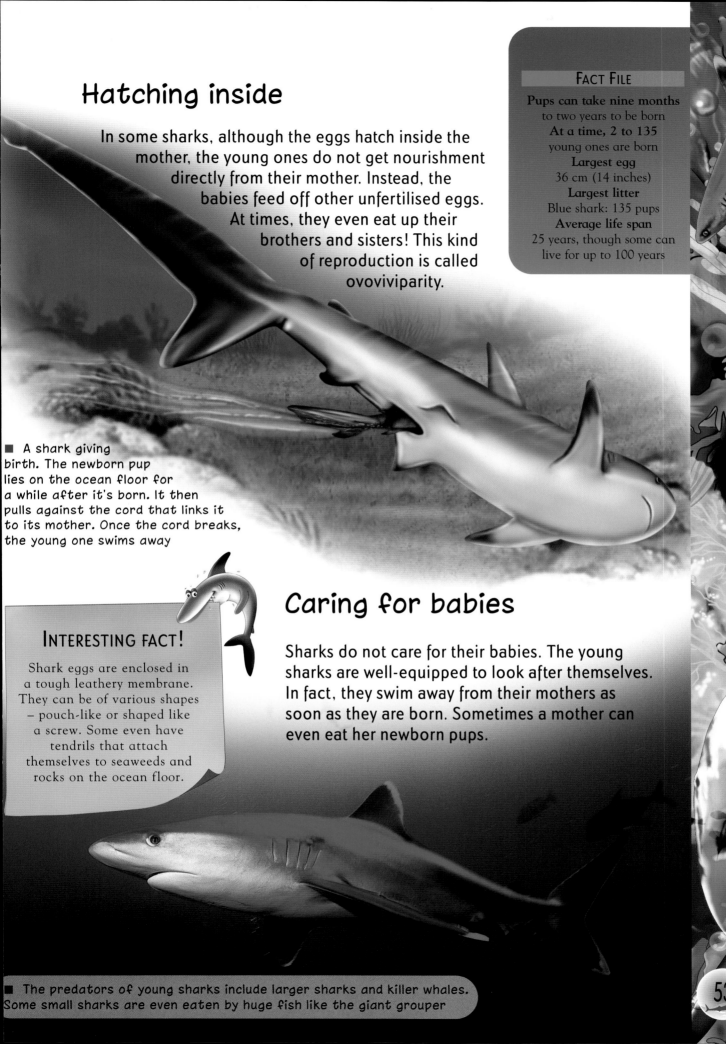

Hatching inside

In some sharks, although the eggs hatch inside the mother, the young ones do not get nourishment directly from their mother. Instead, the babies feed off other unfertilised eggs. At times, they even eat up their brothers and sisters! This kind of reproduction is called ovoviviparity.

■ A shark giving birth. The newborn pup lies on the ocean floor for a while after it's born. It then pulls against the cord that links it to its mother. Once the cord breaks, the young one swims away

INTERESTING FACT!

Shark eggs are enclosed in a tough leathery membrane. They can be of various shapes – pouch-like or shaped like a screw. Some even have tendrils that attach themselves to seaweeds and rocks on the ocean floor.

Caring for babies

Sharks do not care for their babies. The young sharks are well-equipped to look after themselves. In fact, they swim away from their mothers as soon as they are born. Sometimes a mother can even eat her newborn pups.

■ The predators of young sharks include larger sharks and killer whales. Some small sharks are even eaten by huge fish like the giant grouper

Giants of the Deep

Huge sharks have dominated the oceans of the world for centuries. Although the largest sharks today do not compare in size to the Megalodon they can still grow to enormous sizes. Amongst the modern sharks, the largest are the whale shark and basking shark.

Not a whale!

Contrary to what its name suggests, the whale shark is not a whale. It is a shark that can grow to the length of a bus! The whale shark has a huge mouth that may measure up to 1m (4 feet).

Straining food

Whale sharks and basking sharks feed on plankton by straining the tiny marine plants and animals from the water. They swim with their mouth open and suck in water filled with plankton. The shark then filters its food through special bristles attached to the gills and swallows the food. The water is ejected through the gill slits.

INTERESTING FACT!

Both whale sharks and basking sharks are slow swimmers. They swim by moving their body from side to side. Neither of these sharks is a danger to humans.

Whale shark

Colourful skins

Whale sharks have light-grey skin with yellow dots and stripes. On the other hand, basking sharks are darker in colour. They are greyish-brown to black or bluish on the upper surface, while their belly is off-white in colour.

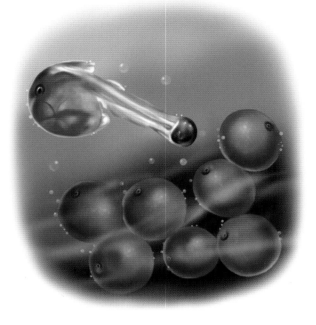

■ Whale sharks love fish eggs. They are known to wait for hours for fish to lay eggs so that they can eat them. They even return year after year to the same mating grounds where the fish release their eggs into the water

The big basking

The basking shark is the second-largest shark. It has a short and conical snout. Unlike whale sharks that travel alone, basking sharks often move around in schools of 100 members.

■ Basking sharks are so called because they cruise slowly along the ocean surface. This gives them the appearance of basking in the sun

Pygmies of the Deep

Not all sharks are huge monsters. Some are, in fact, so small that they can fit into your hand! The smallest sharks include the pygmy ribbontail catshark, dwarf lanternshark and the spined pygmy shark. But like their bigger siblings, small sharks have strong teeth, and a bite from them can be decidedly painful!

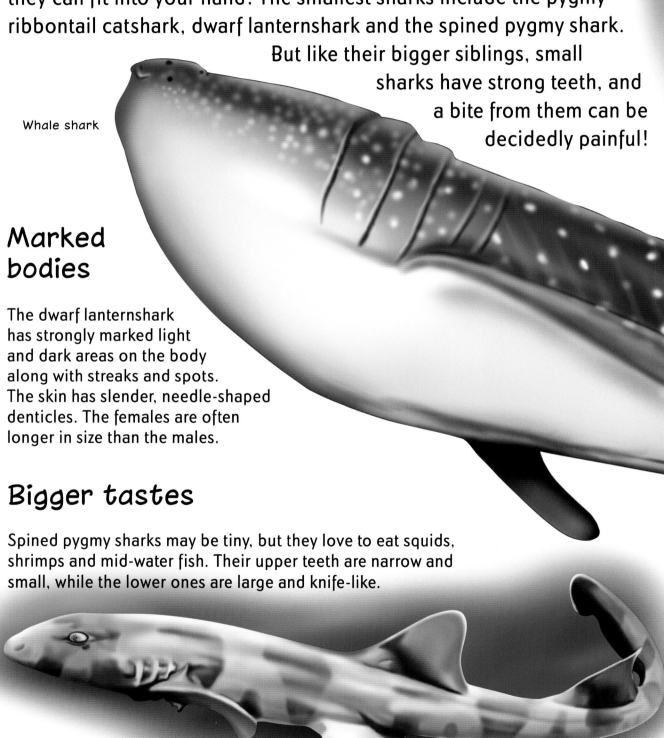

Whale shark

Marked bodies

The dwarf lanternshark has strongly marked light and dark areas on the body along with streaks and spots. The skin has slender, needle-shaped denticles. The females are often longer in size than the males.

Bigger tastes

Spined pygmy sharks may be tiny, but they love to eat squids, shrimps and mid-water fish. Their upper teeth are narrow and small, while the lower ones are large and knife-like.

■ The Freycinet's epaulette is a tiny shark found in the coral reefs of Papua New Guinea. It hides during the day and hunts at night

Tiny and glowing

Spined pygmy sharks are very sleek and have a bulb-like snout. They are dark grey to black in colour and have white-tipped fins. Their bellies actually glow in the dark. They live in deep waters and are rarely seen.

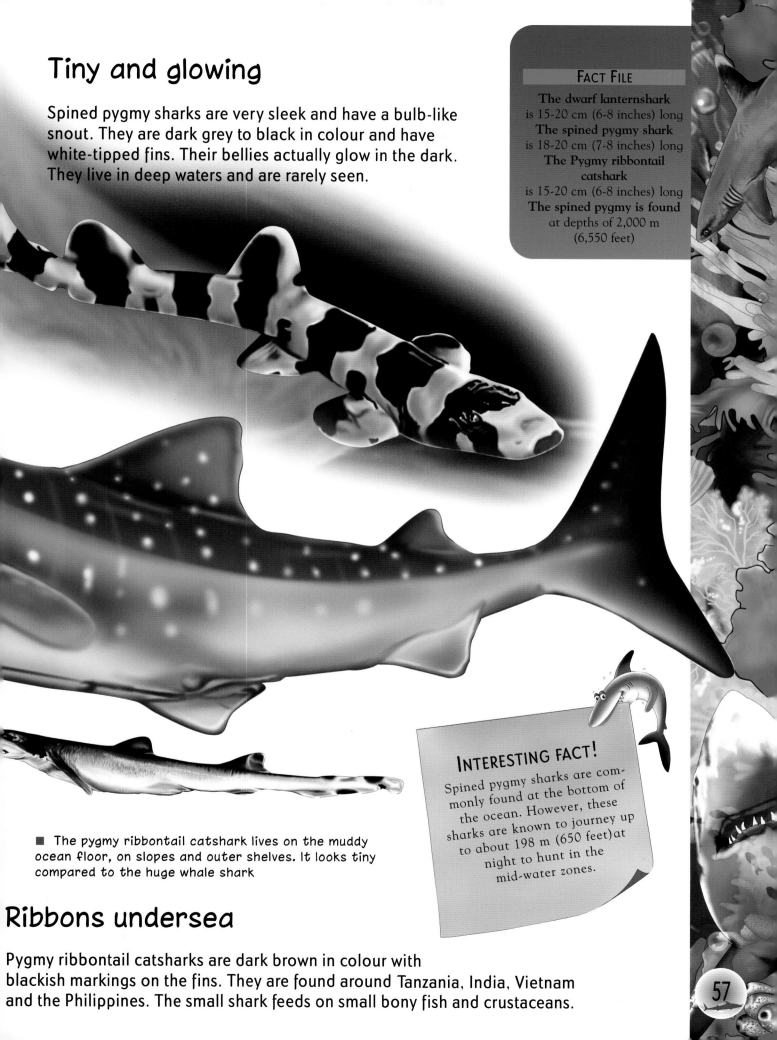

■ The pygmy ribbontail catshark lives on the muddy ocean floor, on slopes and outer shelves. It looks tiny compared to the huge whale shark

INTERESTING FACT!

Spined pygmy sharks are commonly found at the bottom of the ocean. However, these sharks are known to journey up to about 198 m (650 feet) at night to hunt in the mid-water zones.

Ribbons undersea

Pygmy ribbontail catsharks are dark brown in colour with blackish markings on the fins. They are found around Tanzania, India, Vietnam and the Philippines. The small shark feeds on small bony fish and crustaceans.

The Great White Shark

Infamous for its appearance in the movie *Jaws* as a bloodthirsty man-eater, the great white shark is the largest predatory shark. The name *Jaws* was apt, given that this shark has as many as 3,000 razor-sharp teeth! It grows to over 4.5 m (14.7 feet) in length and weighs as much as 1,360 kg (3,000 pounds)! The great white is also known as the "white pointer" and "white death".

Where are they found?

Great white sharks live in temperate to warm waters. They are found across the world – from the coasts of America, the Gulf, Hawaii, South Africa and West Africa to Sandinavia, the Mediterranean Sea, Australia, New Zealand, Japan, and the eastern coastline of China and southern Russia.

Colour that helps

The great white is actually grey or bluish-grey in colour, with a white underbelly. Its colouring helps it to get close to its prey without being noticed. When seen from below, the white underbelly blends in with the bright reflection of the sky. Quite often, this shark attacks its victims by sneaking up quietly. The shark's greyish colour then helps it to blend in with the dark water.

■ Great white sharks are solitary creatures and prefer to swim alone. However, they have sometimes been sighted in pairs

Fierce bite

With a mouth that is most often open, you cannot miss the rows of white, triangle-shaped, razor-sharp teeth. The shark's teeth can grow up to 7.5 cm (3 inches) long. Old or broken teeth are replaced by a row of new teeth.

FACT FILE

Average length
3.6-4.9 m (12-16 feet)
Can grow up to
6.8 m (22.3 feet)
Can be as heavy as
3,312 kg (7,302 pounds)
Number of babies
2-14 pups
Shark attack
30-50 attacks per year
Fatal attacks
10-15 deaths every year
Can swim as deep as
250 m (775 feet)

INTERESTING FACT!

Great white sharks are ovoviviparous. The eggs of the great white remain inside the body of the female shark until they hatch. The female then gives birth to live young ones.

■ Great white sharks often jump out of the water while chasing seals. This is called breaching

What do they eat?

Great whites eat dolphins, sea lions, seals, big bony fish and even penguins. Though they have earned a reputation for being man-eaters, they do not usually attack humans. These sharks are also scavengers, as they eat dead animals that float in water.

The great white first attacks its victim, injures it and then moves away. It approaches it later, when the pain and bleeding has weakened it. The shark does not chew its food, but rips the prey into mouth-sized pieces before swallowing them. After a good meal, the shark can do without another one for over a month!

■ Great whites are known to attack pelicans, but they prefer to eat seals

Tiger Sharks and Bull Sharks

Many sharks, like the tiger and bull sharks, are named after land animals. The tiger shark has dark stripes on its back, similar to the big cat. But as the shark grows older, the stripes often fade away. The bull shark gets its name from its flat, wide and short snout, which resembles that of a bull.

■ Tiger sharks have good eyesight, which is aided by a special gill slit called a spiracle. Located behind the eye, this slit provides oxygen directly to the eyes and the brain

Tough tigers

The tiger shark has a very large mouth with powerful jaws. The triangular teeth of these sharks have saw-like edges that can slice through many objects. The tiger shark is not a very fast swimmer and often hunts at night.

Junk eaters

Tiger sharks love food and will eat almost anything. Biologists have found alarm clocks, tin cans, deer antlers and even shoes in the stomach of dead tiger sharks! Tiger sharks also feed on other sharks, fish, turtles and crabs.

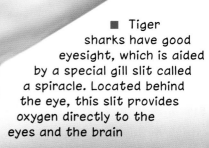

■ Tiger sharks often prey on albatross chicks, which fall into the ocean while learning to fly

Bull sharks

The bull shark lives near coastal areas. It is also commonly found in rivers and freshwater lakes. Bull sharks eat fish, other sharks, turtles, birds and dolphins. Interestingly, adult female bull sharks are longer in size than male bull sharks.

Danger zone

It is dangerous to go near bull and tiger sharks, as they are known to be man-eaters. Tiger sharks are the second-most threatening species to humans, after the great white. Bull sharks rank third in this respect.

INTERESTING FACT!

Bull sharks travel from the upper Amazon River to the sea every season. They cover a distance of 3,700 km (2,300 miles) during this journey.

■ Bull sharks hardly have any predators. But there have been reports of crocodiles eating bull sharks

61

The Swift Mako

Sharks are great swimmers, and the fastest among them is the mako. The mako's speed has been recorded at 31 mph (50 km/h). The mako is renowned for its ability to leap out of the water, to heights of up to 6 m (20 ft). They have even been known to jump into boats!

Shaped for speed

Makos are fast swimmers because of their sleek, spindle-like shape. They also have a long and conical snout. Their side fins are short and the tail fin is crescent-shaped to provide more power while swimming.

Other relatives

Makos belong to the order of mackerel sharks. Other sharks in this order include the great white, the porbeagle and the sand tiger shark. Sand tiger sharks are also called grey nurse sharks. They are found in most warm seas around the world. The porbeagle gets its name from its porpoise-like shape.

■ The sand tiger shark is known to swim to the surface and take huge gulps of air. It holds the air in its stomach to lie motionless in the water

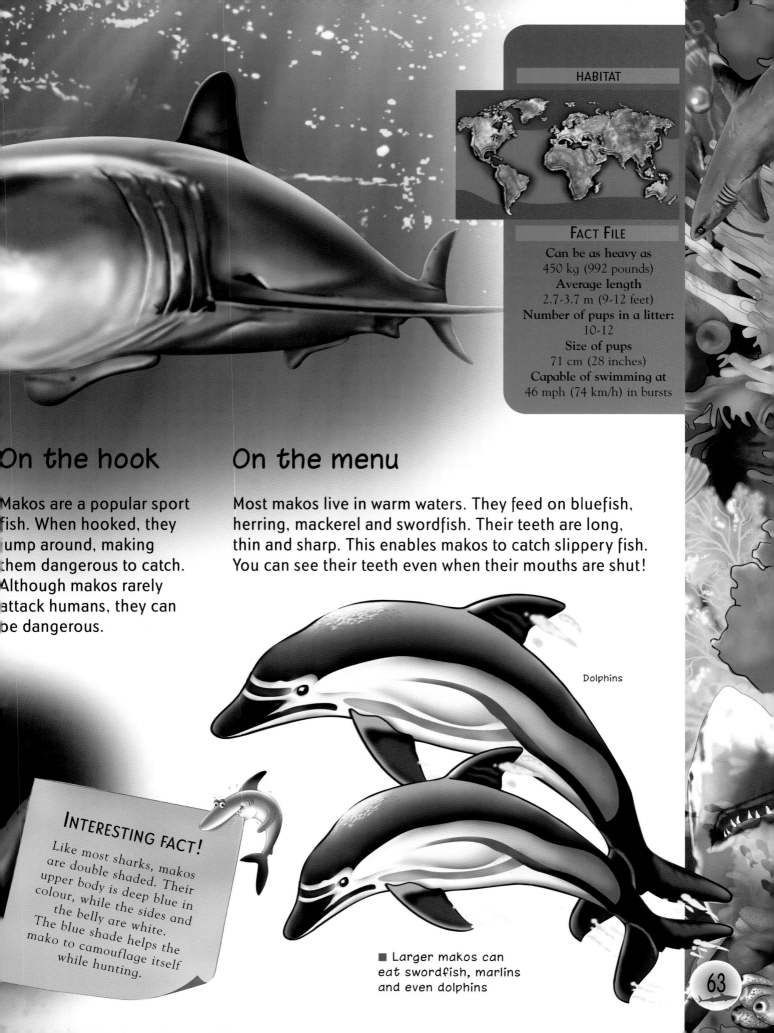

FACT FILE

Can be as heavy as
450 kg (992 pounds)
Average length
2.7-3.7 m (9-12 feet)
Number of pups in a litter:
10-12
Size of pups
71 cm (28 inches)
Capable of swimming at
46 mph (74 km/h) in bursts

On the hook

Makos are a popular sport fish. When hooked, they jump around, making them dangerous to catch. Although makos rarely attack humans, they can be dangerous.

On the menu

Most makos live in warm waters. They feed on bluefish, herring, mackerel and swordfish. Their teeth are long, thin and sharp. This enables makos to catch slippery fish. You can see their teeth even when their mouths are shut!

Dolphins

INTERESTING FACT!

Like most sharks, makos are double shaded. Their upper body is deep blue in colour, while the sides and the belly are white. The blue shade helps the mako to camouflage itself while hunting.

■ Larger makos can eat swordfish, marlins and even dolphins

63

Ground Sharks

Ground sharks are the most common type of sharks. They have long snouts and a mouth that reaches behind the eyes. Their eyes are special too. Ground shark eyes have a lower eyelid that moves to cover the eyes during hunting. Ground sharks include hammerhead, carpet and swell sharks and all the requiem sharks, such as the tiger, blue, lemon, bull and certain reef sharks.

Lemon shark

Yellow fellows

The lemon shark gets its name from its deep yellow brown colour. But its belly is off-white. This shark hunts mostly at night. During the day, it loves to laze on the ocean floor.

Blue moods

The blue shark has a slim body that is deep blue on the back, bright blue on the sides and white on the belly. They also have slender snouts and large eyes. They are the second-fastest swimmers after the mako. While there were once many blue sharks in the ocean, over-fishing has led to a drop in their population.

■ The nictitating membrane of the blue shark helps it to protect its eyes during hunting

64

■ The swell shark can increase the size of its body by swallowing large amounts of water. This scares away the shark's enemies

Danger factor

Lemon sharks live near the surface and are often seen at bays, docks and river mouths. Though they swim close to human areas, lemon sharks attack only if provoked. Meanwhile, blue sharks live far away from the shores, and yet are known to attack humans.

INTERESTING FACT!

The blue shark migrates the longest distances. It travels 2,000-3,000 km (1,200-1,700 miles) in a seasonal journey from New York State in the US to Brazil.

■ While most sharks eat other sea animals, Californian sea lions love to feed on young blue sharks

No fuss about food

Blue sharks can eat anything, but they prefer squid and fish. On the other hand, the lemon shark likes to feed on crabs, rays, shrimps, sea birds and smaller sharks.

Reef Sharks

Sharks live in different zones and regions of the ocean. Some, such as blacktip, whitetip and Caribbean reef sharks, live near coral reefs. Divers and waders often come into contact with such sharks.

■ Whitetip reef sharks are viviparous. A single litter could contain between one and five pups. Each pup is around 61 cm (24 inches) long

White cousins

The whitetip reef shark is grey in colour, with white tips on its dorsal fin and tail. It is slender and has a broad head. It feeds mainly on bony fish, octopuses, lobsters and crabs.

■ The whitetip reef shark is often confuse with the silvertip shar However, the silvertip much heavier, and its is lined with white, rather than tipped, as it is in the whitetip

ar
on t
s, ray

Sleepy sharks

Caribbean reef sharks live near the coral reefs of the Caribbean. These sharks often appear to be asleep, as they lie motionless at the bottom of the ocean. They love to feed on bony fish.

The blacktip

The blacktip reef shark is very interesting to look at. Its body is grey in colour, but the tips of its fins are black. The shark also has a white streak on its side. The blacktip reef shark thrives in aquariums.

INTERESTING FACT!

Whitetip reef sharks are most active at night, when they roam the reef in search of food. During the day, the shark rests in coral caves. Whitetips rest in groups, but they hunt alone.

■ Unlike other sharks, the silky shark has smooth skin. This is because the teeth-like scales are closely packed. Although silky sharks are largely found in deep oceans, they also frequent deepwater reefs

Living zones

Reef sharks live in different areas and depths of the ocean. The blacktip reef shark is found on sand flats at depths of 15 m (49.2 feet). The whitetip prefers to live in corners and caves around coral reefs.

67

Angelsharks

Angelsharks have flat bodies, which make them look very much like rays. They often bury themselves in sand or mud, leaving just their eyes and the tops of their bodies protruding.

Eye

Spiracle

Pectoral fin

Winged sharks

Angelsharks have long, wide fins that look like wings which is why they are called angelsharks. They have a blunt snout, and their skin colour is similar to that of the sand and rocks found in the ocean. This helps them to hide from their prey or enemies.

Pelvic fin

■ Both angelsharks and rays give birth to young ones. They also have similar flat bodies. But unlike rays, the fins of the angelshark are not attached to the sides of its head

68

FACT FILE

Can grow up to
2 m (6.5 feet)
Number of babies
8-13 pups
Found at depths of up to
1,300 m (4,300 feet)
Can be as heavy as
27 kg (60 pounds)
Pups born at depths of
18.3-27.4 m (60-90 feet)

Hunting by surprise

The angelshark hides in the sand and rocks,
waiting for its prey. As a fish swims by, the shark
pounces on it suddenly. The angelshark eats
fish, crustaceans and molluscs.
It has small and sharp teeth.

First dorsal fin

Second dorsal fin

Caudal fin

INTERESTING FACT!

Angelsharks are not really dangerous if left in peace. But they can bite if you step on them. That's why they are sometimes called sand devils!

Bottom dwellers

Angelsharks live at the
bottom of the ocean
and prefer warm waters.
They are mostly found in
the Pacific and Atlantic
Oceans. Angelsharks
are not fast swimmers,
but their prey is often
even slower!

■ The angelshark feeds on a
variety of reef fish including
croakers, groupers and flatfish

69

Hammerheads

Hammerhead sharks are unique creatures, and can be easily spotted, even from a distance. They have a flat and rectangular head, which resembles a hammer. There are many types of hammerhead sharks. They can be differentiated by the shape of their heads.

Heady features

The eyes of the hammerhead shark are placed at the ends of its distinct head. The eyes can be as far apart as 1 m (3.3 feet), allowing the shark to view a larger area. Its flat head also helps the shark to keep its balance, as its side fins are very short.

Hammerhead Eye

Little differences

The great hammerhead has a straight head with a slight notch in the centre. The scalloped hammerhead has rounded corners on its head, while the smooth hammerhead has a broad and flat head without a notch. The bonnethead is smaller, with a shovel-shaped head.

■ The upper side of the hammerhead is dark brown, light grey or even olive in colour, while its belly is white

70

■ The great hammerhead migrates seasonally, moving to cooler waters during the summer

Home sweet home

Hammerheads can be found across many areas. They can live at depths of 300 m (984 feet) and can also be found in shallow coastal areas, including lagoons. They are usually found in the Mediterranean Sea and the Atlantic, Pacific and Indian Oceans.

INTERESTING FACT!

Angelfish act as official cleaners to hammerhead sharks. They pick up parasites from the sharks' skin and even inside their mouths. Interestingly, the hammerhead does not eat these cleaners!

Stingray

Meal time

Hammerhead sharks eat crabs and fish. But their favourite food is stingray. The shark pins the stingray down using its "hammer". It feeds after sundown and hunts along the seafloor as well as near the surface. Large hammerheads also eat smaller ones.

Sharks with a Difference

The world under the ocean is a curious place. It is home to many living creatures of all shapes, colours and sizes. Sharks, too, belong to this wonderful world. Ornate wobbegongs, carpet sharks and horn sharks are just some of the odd members of the shark family.

■ The horn shark is not considered to be dangerous to people, but the spines can hurt if the shark is handled

The horned pig

The horn shark has a short and blunt head, and looks very much like a pig! It is either grey or brown in colour, with dark spots covering its body. The shark's small teeth are located in the front of its jaw, with large crushing molars along the sides. It is most active at night and feeds on sea urchins, crabs, worms and anemones.

The ornate ocean creature

The ornate wobbegong lives in the Australian and Pacific coastal reefs. It is called ornate because its skin has patterns in brown, yellow and grey colours. This helps the shark to blend into its surroundings.

Baiting for food

The wobbegong has worm-like projections around its mouth. The shark uses these to suck its prey into the mouth. Like the angelshark, the wobbegong also surprises its victims by camouflaging itself at the bottom of the ocean.

■ This varied carpet shark is a relative of the whale shark. But there are very few similarities between the two. The varied carpet shark is small and has a distinctive black `collar` with white spots

INTERESTING FACT!

The horn shark's egg cases are curiously shaped in a spiral, like a screw. Each case contains one pup and takes from six to nine months to hatch.

The ornate wobbegong

Goblins in water

The goblin shark has an unusual snout, which is long, flat and pointed. The jaws point out when the shark eats, making it look very peculiar indeed! It has soft, pale and pinkish-grey skin.

■ Little is known about goblin sharks, but it is believed that they are slow swimmers

All in the Family

Sharks have many relatives in the ocean. One of their closest cousins is the ray. Sharks and rays actually had the same ancestors about 200 million years ago.

■ Skates and rays are very similar to look at. The main difference between them lies in their method of reproduction. Rays are viviparous, while skates lay eggs

Body matters

The biggest difference between sharks and rays lies in body shape. While sharks have long slender bodies, rays have flattened ones. But some sharks, like angelsharks, have bodies like those of rays.

Gill slits

Similar features

Sharks and rays have many common features. Both have skeletons made of cartilage and skins covered with denticles. Both sharks and rays have between five and seven gill slits. However, a shark's gill slits are on either side of its head, while a ray's gill slits are on the underside of its body.

■ Manta rays are scary to look at and are often called devil rays. But in reality, manta rays are playful and splash around in the water!

Swimming skills

Sea creatures have different styles of swimming. For instance, rays flap their big side fins in order to swim. But sharks use their much smaller fins just for lifting and steering. They use their tails to move around in water.

■ The saw of a young sawfish is covered in a protective membrane to avoid hurting the mother when she gives birth

Name game

Like most big families, sharks and their relatives have similar names, as do sawfish and sawsharks. But often, there is very little similarity between the two. For example, the sawshark is brown, while the sawfish is light blue in colour. Moreover, the sawfish does not have barbels in the middle of its "saw".

INTERESTING FACT!
Many rays have spines on their tails, which can sting other animals. These spines can be poisonous too. Some rays have long and whip-like tails, while others have shorter ones.

75

Shark Attack!

Over the years, shark attacks have caught the imagination of filmmakers and fiction writers. The image of a shark with its huge mouth wide open, flashing its deadly teeth, has thrilled many a movie-goer. But not all sharks are a threat to us. In fact, most sharks will not attack humans!

Not always deadly

Usually, shark attacks do not result in death or serious injury. Sharks only attack humans out of fear. Some attacks are also by accident, when a shark mistakes human surfers for seals!

■ It is not a good idea to swim with an open wound, as the smell of blood attracts sharks

Be careful

Nevertheless, one has to be careful while swimming in shark-inhabited waters. One should always swim during the day and in a group. Leave the water immediately if a shark is spotted, but do so quietly. And never try to grab a shark, even if it is a small one!

ANNUAL DATA

Total shark attacks
75-100
Unprovoked attacks
Around 50
Provoked attacks
15-20
Fatal attacks
11-15
Most number of attacks
recorded in:
US (over 30 attacks
every year)

■ Sharks are curious animals. They will survey a man in a cage, even though they cannot attack him!

Warning bells

If you upset a shark by trespassing in its territory, it usually warns you before attacking. It shakes its head and swims with its back hunched and snout pointing up. This is called agonistic display. If such movements are seen, one should swim away before it's too late.

INTERESTING FACT!

People are more likely to die from bee stings or dog bites than to be killed by sharks! In fact, more than 90 per cent of those attacked by sharks manage to survive.

Most dangerous

There are four sharks that are particularly dangerous to humans. These are the great white, tiger, bull and oceanic whitetip sharks. Seventeen other types of sharks have also attacked humans, but they are dangerous only if threatened or disturbed. These include lemon, hammerhead, blacktip reef, nurse, wobbegong, sandtiger and spitting sharks.

■ California has one of the highest attack rates by the great white in the world, but deaths are very rare. Most of the attacks are on surfers and divers

77

Endangered Sharks

Sharks are the kings of the oceans as they have no natural predators. They are often scary in appearance and have a reputation as being ruthless hunters. But today, sharks have much to fear from humans. Different parts of sharks, like the skin, fins and flesh, are used for various purposes.

In danger

Due to the wide-scale killing of sharks, there has been a drop in the shark population. In fact, many have become endangered. They are so few in number that if we don't stop hunting them certain species could become extinct. To protect such sharks, many countries have made it illegal to kill sharks.

Just a bycatch

Some sharks are caught by accident, as ships and fishermen try to catch other fish. A shark caught in this manner is called a bycatch. People are now working on ways to stop these accidental killings.

INTERESTING FACT!

You can adopt a shark! Adopted sharks are specially tagged, so that you can track their movements. Shark adoption is a great way to support and protect sharks.

■ Sharks usually attack us only if we disturb them, but humans follow and hunt sharks even as a sport

Many a product

Sharks are used in a variety of man-made products. Shark scales are removed from the skin and the hide is used to make luxurious leather.
The liver oil of some sharks contains large amounts of Vitamin A. Until the late 1940s, such sharks were hunted in large numbers for Vitamin A.

■ Shark-liver oil contains more Vitamin A than cod-liver oil

■ Shark-liver oil is even used in the manufacture of lipsticks and other cosmetics

Soupy tales

The Chinese use dried shark fins to make a popular and expensive soup. The best soup is considered a highly prized delicacy and some top restaurants charge as much as US $100 a bowl!

■ Fins used in soups are often obtained in a cruel manner. In some countries fishermen drag living sharks from the sea and slice off their fins and tails. The wounded sharks are then thrown back into the water, where they bleed to death

Under the Sea

Whales are warm-blooded underwater mammals
that can be found all over the world.

Where Do They Come From?

Whales belong to the order Cetacea and are descended from land mammals that belonged to the order Artiodactyl, or even-toed ungulates. It is believed that they first ventured into the waters about 50 million years ago. The Basilosaurus and Dorudon were fully aquatic creatures recognisable as whales.

What Do They Look Like?

Whales are warm-blooded sea mammals that breathe through lungs rather than gills. They are usually black, grey, tan or white in colour. A thick layer of fat, known as blubber, underlies the inside of their skin. There are two main types of whales, Baleen and Toothed.

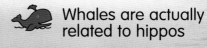 Whales are actually related to hippos

Fun Fact

Hind limbs have disappeared in whales due to evolution, but many whales still retain remnants of their forelimbs.

The tail fins, or flukes, help the whales to move in water

Are They In Danger?

Whales have very few natural predators. In fact, humans pose the greatest threat to their survival. For centuries, whales have been hunted for their meat, bone, blubber and oil. This is known as whaling and has resulted in a widespread decline in their numbers. Harmful human activities, like the contamination of the oceans with toxins and industrial waste, as well as the use of sonar by ships and submarines, put whales and other sea creatures in danger.

Many modern ships use sonar to navigate, which is thought to be harmful to whales

Mammals

Although whales look like fish, they are actually mammals and have distinct mammal-like features.

 Whales have tiny bristles around their mouths that help them to feel things

Mammal Features

All whales are warm-blooded mammals. This means that they produce and regulate their own heat in their body. Whales also breathe through their lungs with the help of blowholes located at the top of their heads. Like land mammals, female whales give birth to live young and nurse them on milk until they can feed for themselves.

 Beluga whales have a heart rate of 12-20 beats per minute

My Heart Is Beating

Another characteristic that whales share with all mammals is that they have four-chambered hearts. Their heart rate differs between species; large whales usually have a slower heart rate than smaller ones, averaging around 10-30 beats per minute. They are known to lower their heart rates when diving into deep waters. This prevents excess loss of oxygen during the process.

Fun Fact

Whales use muscles in their forestomachs to chew their food.

How They Are Different

Whales may be mammals in the true sense, but they have many distinct features that they do not share with other mammals. They have no bones to support their dorsal fins. They have forward extending jaws and their upper jaw is moved backwards so that the blowhole is at the top of their head. Whales also do not possess skin glands, a sense of smell or tear glands and their ears have no outward openings.

Whales are quite different from other aquatic mammals, such as sea lions and manatees

Whale Senses

Whales have adapted their senses to life under and on the surface of the water.

 Sight is not as important as hearing in the dark underwater world

The Five Senses

Whales are able to see underwater, but their sight is not as well-developed as their sense of hearing. This is because sound carries better under water than over land. Whale skin is very sensitive to touch. A whale's sense of taste is a subject of great debate among scientists. Their sense of smell is very poor, indeed most whales have no sense of smell at all.

 It is believed that the Earth's magnetic field helps guide whales during migration

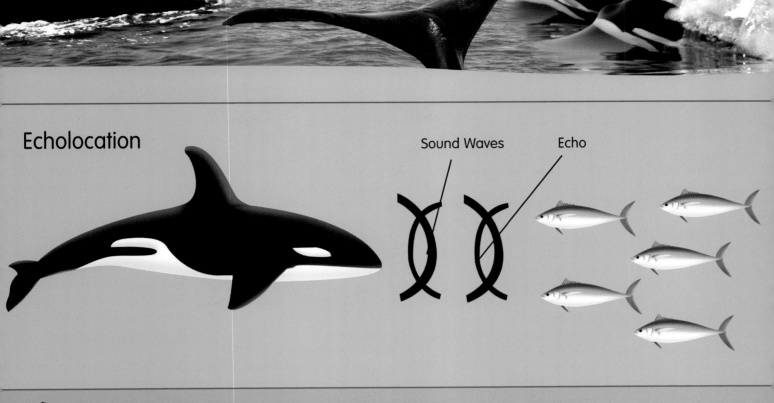

Echolocation

Sound Waves   Echo

 Whales use echolocation to find their way underwater. They also use it to detect predators, prey and any other kind of danger that may lie ahead of them

Echolocation

Whales possess a highly developed sense of hearing. In this they are aided by their ability to echolocate. Echolocation is a complex process in which whales emit clicking sounds which are channeled by a fat-filled, melon-shaped organ in their head. The sound bounces off an object and comes back to the whale in the form of an echo. Whales receive this sound in a cavity full of fat in their lower jaw. From there it is sent to the brain. Echolocation helps whales to understand the shape, distance, texture and location of different objects.

Fun Fact

Echolocation is better developed in Toothed whales than in Baleen whales.

Magnetic Personality

Whales possess another special ability. It is believed that they can detect the magnetic field of the Earth and use this to navigate during long migrations. It is, however, not clear how they are able to do this. Some scientists believe that when whales become stranded on beaches it is because an abnormality the Earth's magnetic field has drawn them there.

Whale Sounds

The sounds made by whales, in order to communicate and for other purposes, are known as whale song.

The most haunting sounds are made by Humpack whales

Why Do They Sing?

The sense of hearing is very important to whales because they depend on it for almost all their daily activities. This is mainly because their other senses are not as effective underwater as sound. Whales use sound for communication, echolocation and navigation. It also helps them to detect the depth of water and the shape and size of an obstacle.

Toothed Whales

Toothed whales have a more complex system of sound production than Baleen whales. High-frequency clicks and whistles are produced through a narrow passage in their head known as the phonic lips. Air passing through here causes the tissues to vibrate, producing a sound. Most whales have two sets of phonic lips and can produce two different sounds.

Baleen Whales

Unlike Toothed whales, Baleen whales do not possess phonic lips. The larynx is used instead, much the same as humans, but the mechanism is not exactly like ours. They probably recycle air within their bodies to produce sound. There is still no clear information on their sound-producing mechanism.

Fun Fact

Toothed whales produce sounds that range between 10-31,000 Hz.

 Baleen whales use their larynx to produce sound

 Sound producing mechanism in Dolphins and Toothed whales

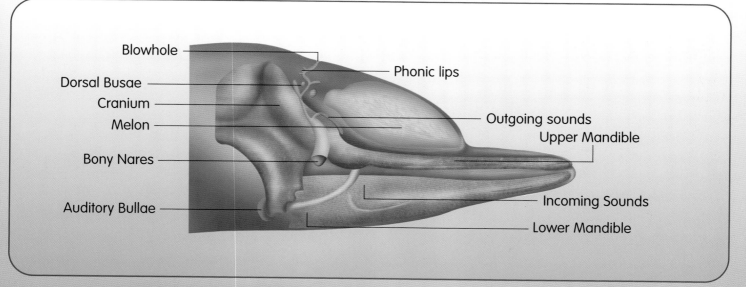

Blowhole

Phonic lips

Dorsal Busae

Cranium

Melon

Outgoing sounds

Upper Mandible

Bony Nares

Auditory Bullae

Incoming Sounds

Lower Mandible

No Sleep

Like all mammals, whales need sleep and they have specially adapted their sleeping habits to suit their environment.

Why Can't They Sleep?

Whales have a respiratory system that is quite different from land mammals. It is not an involuntary action. Instead, they actually breathe at will. Moreover, because they live underwater, they must keep moving at all times to prevent themselves from sinking to the bottom of the sea. As a result, whales cannot reach a deep sleep, otherwise they would drown!

Whales need to keep swimming so that they do not sink to the bottom

Beauty Sleep

Their inabilty to sleep deeply does not mean that whales do not sleep at all. In fact, they require 8 hours of sleep each day. They are able to do so by letting only one part of their brain sleep while keeping the other part awake. It is believed that some Toothed whales actually sleep in large groups, where one member stays completely awake, and has the task of reminding the others to breathe.

Baleen whales can sleep comfortably while floating on the surface

Whales usually have very light and dreamless sleep

Are You Dreaming?

An interesting question is whether whales dream in their sleep. EEG sleep tests have been performed on whales by scientists. This test studies stages of sleep. It has been observed that whales rarely go into the REM, or Rapid Eye Movement, stage of sleep. This is the level at which humans normally dream. This suggests that whales have very light sleep, probably without any dreams.

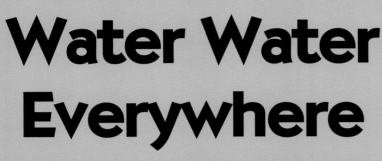

Water Water Everywhere

A long time ago whales, dolphins and porpoises were land animals. Over the course of millions of years they adapted themselves to live underwater.

Body of A Swimmer

Whales have many special features that are well adapted for swimming underwater. Their bodies are streamlined in order to reduce friction with the water. They have very little hair on them, which also reduces friction. Whales have very flexible rib cages that, in some cases, are completely free and unattached from the spinal column. This enables the chest to open out wide and let in more air while breathing.

 Whales have specially designed bone structures that help them to swim

 Whales have streamlined bodies to reduce friction with the water

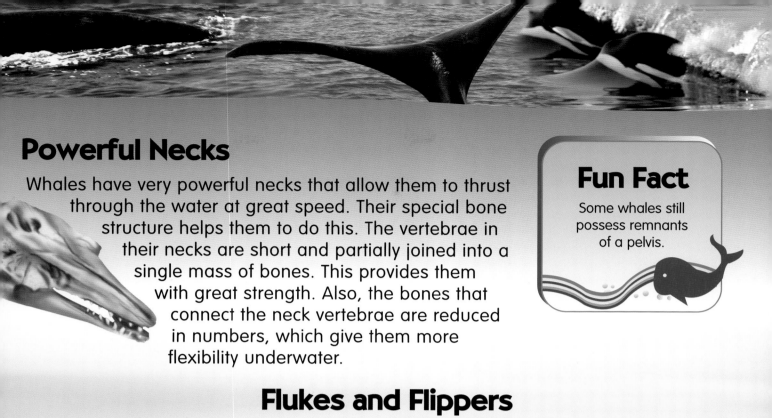

Powerful Necks

Whales have very powerful necks that allow them to thrust through the water at great speed. Their special bone structure helps them to do this. The vertebrae in their necks are short and partially joined into a single mass of bones. This provides them with great strength. Also, the bones that connect the neck vertebrae are reduced in numbers, which give them more flexibility underwater.

Fun Fact

Some whales still possess remnants of a pelvis.

Flukes and Flippers

Whales use the horizontal flukes in their tails to propel themselves through the water. Flippers are used for steering. These are made up of short and flat arm bones, several elongated fingers and disc-like wrist bones. The joint at their elbow is almost fixed in one place, making their flippers rigid. All these features help them to swim efficiently.

Whales have almost rigid flippers, that help them to steer in water

Heat Regulation

The world's oceans can be extremely cold, which is why whales have to be well protected in order to keep themselves warm.

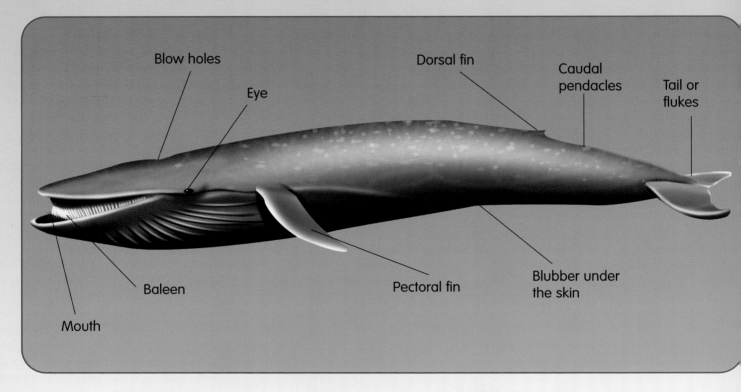

Blow holes

Eye

Dorsal fin

Caudal pendacles

Tail or flukes

Baleen

Mouth

Pectoral fin

Blubber under the skin

 The blubber is a layer of fat under the skin

Effective Insulation

The most effective protection against the cold that whales have is their blubber. This is a thick layer of fat found under the skin. It runs across their whole body except for their flippers and flukes. The blubber acts as an insulatory layer, which prevents body heat from escaping, conserving heat. Blubber is also used to store energy for when food is scarce.

Fun Fact

Heat is lost in water around 27 times faster than in air under similar temperatures.

Many sea mammals, such as sea otters, have fur instead of blubber

Why Is Blubber Better Than Fur?

Blubber is better at conserving heat than fur. Pockets of air are held by fur and this traps heat. However, when brought under pressure these pockets of air can be released. Blubber retains its level of insulation under pressure.

Whale limbs are small, which helps reduce heat loss

Others Methods of Conserving Heat

The fusiform (tapered at both ends) shape of their body and small sized limbs, minimises the surface area of the whale's extremeties, where the majority of heat is lost, and helps reduce the loss of body heat. Moreover, the whale's circulatory system also helps to regulate body heat by either keeping in or letting out body heat, when necessary.

Feeding Time

There are two types of whales – Toothed and Baleen –
and each type has a different method of feeding.

Filtering Food

Baleen whales are different because they have no teeth. Instead of
teeth they have baleen plates, which act like sieves to filter food
from the water. Baleen whales have two blowholes, from which,
water blows out in a v-shape. The females of the species are
usually larger than the males and they are all generally much
bigger in size than Toothed whales.

Baleen whales use the baleen plates
in their mouth to filter their food

Fun Fact

Sperm whales do not
use their teeth to feed.
Instead they use them
to show anger and
for show!

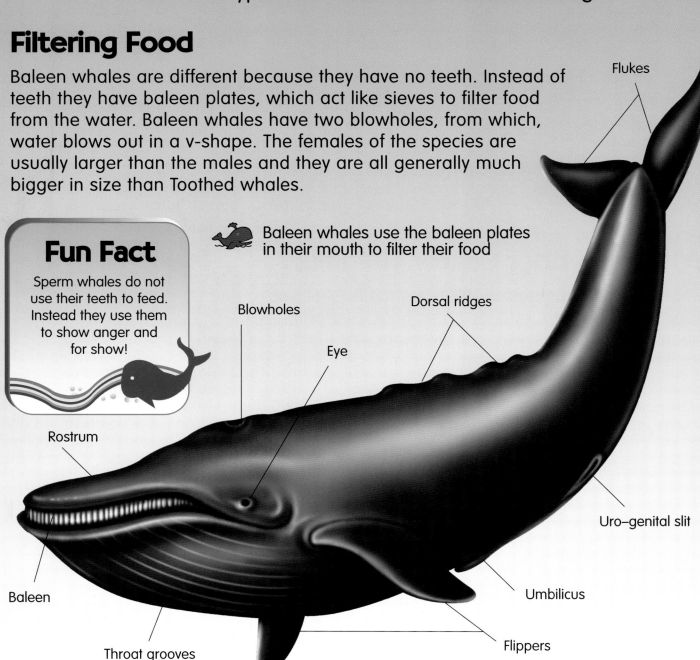

Flukes

Blowholes

Dorsal ridges

Eye

Rostrum

Uro–genital slit

Umbilicus

Baleen

Flippers

Throat grooves

Sinking their Teeth in

Toothed whales are distinguished from Baleen whales by their teeth. These whales are smaller in size and have a single blowhole instead of two. They also have a melon shaped organ on their heads, which has been evolved for echolocation. These whales do not have any vocal cords. Sound is produced by them through their blowholes. They also do not possess any sense of smell or saliva glands. Toothed whales are good hunters. They use their teeth to hold on to their prey. They usually feed on squid, fish and small marine mammals.

Toothed whales have many small conical teeth to catch their prey

Grey whales increase their body weight 16–30% during the feeding season

Time To Eat!

Most whales have a feeding season. Food intake during the feeding season is high, with excess energy being stored as blubber. This blubber sustains the whale during the winter months. Baleen whales spend about four to six months in the summer feeding intensively and the following six to eight months are spent travelling and breeding. During these months they eat much less, if at all.

Deep Breaths

Whales are sea-living mammals and like all mammals breathe oxygen into their lungs, rather than filtering oxygen through gills, like fish.

Blowholes

Whales breathe through their nostrils, which are known as blowholes. These are usually located on the top of their heads and are connected to their lungs through the trachea. Muscular flaps cover the blowholes, which prevent water from entering when submerged and just before a deep dive the strong muscles around the blowholes relax and the flap is allowed to cover them. Sperm whales are known to dive as deep as 9186 ft (2,800 m) for more than 2 hours at a time!

 The blowholes on top of the head allow it to breathe air from the surface

Breathing In and Out

Respiration is not controlled by their autonomic nervous system, but is an act of will for whales which helps them remain underwater for long periods. When whales need air they surface and first blow out the stale air, which is when misty vapour is seen gushing out of the blowholes. They then breathe in fresh air just before diving. The air passes to the lungs, and from there oxygen is carried to the other parts of their body by their blood.

Fun Fact

Unlike humans, whales cannot breathe through their mouths.

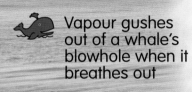

Vapour gushes out of a whale's blowhole when it breathes out

Toothed whales have a single blowhole on top of their heads

How Many Blowholes?

Whales breathe through their blowholes, located at the top of their head. Some whales have one blowhole, while others have two. Most Baleen whales possess two blowholes while Toothed whales usually have just one. This is because in Baleen whales the second blowhole evolved through time to help in echolocation.

Mother Dear

All whales are viviparous mammals, meaning the mother gives birth to the young and nurtures them with her milk.

Whales protect and care for their young ones for a long period of time

Birth

Whales give birth to their young, which are known as calves. Mothers tend to give birth seasonally, and normally a single calf is born every 1–3 years. They prefer giving birth in warm tropical waters and the birth of twins has been known, but is very rare. A whale's gestation period lasts between 9 and 18 months, depending on species.

Young Whales

Newborn whales can swim almost immediately after birth and straight after birth their natural instinct is to head up to the surface of the water to breathe. Calves usually feed on their mother's milk and some whales are known to nurse their offspring for up to a year. Young whales often have a mottled colouration as camouflage, protecting them from predators. Newborn whales can have a light covering of hair, but this is usually lost as they grow older.

Whale calves are born with open eyes and alert senses. They swim up to the surface immediately after birth to breathe

Big and Blue

Blue whales give birth to the largest young of any creature in the world. These huge babies are usually around 7.6 m (25 ft) in length and 5.4–7.3 tonnes (6–8 tons) in weight. The Blue whale's gestation period lasts between 11–12 months, and they give birth every 2–3 years. Baby Blue whales are fed up to 200 litres (50 gallons) of milk every day and they gain about 44 kg (100 lbs) in weight daily!

 The milk of the female Blue whale is very rich in fat

Types of Whales

All whales belong to the order Cetacea. As we've discovered, there are two main types of whales – Baleen and Toothed.

Baleen Whales

Baleen whales seive their food from the water. Baleen whales make up the Mysticeti suborder of Cetacea. For such enormous creatures, a Baleen whale's diet is actually composed of tiny creatures. They feed mainly on krill, which are shrimp-like crustaceans and are consumed in vast quantities.

Fun Fact

Blue whales have 320 pairs of baleen plates and dark grey bristles.

 Baleen whales are usually larger in size than Toothed whales

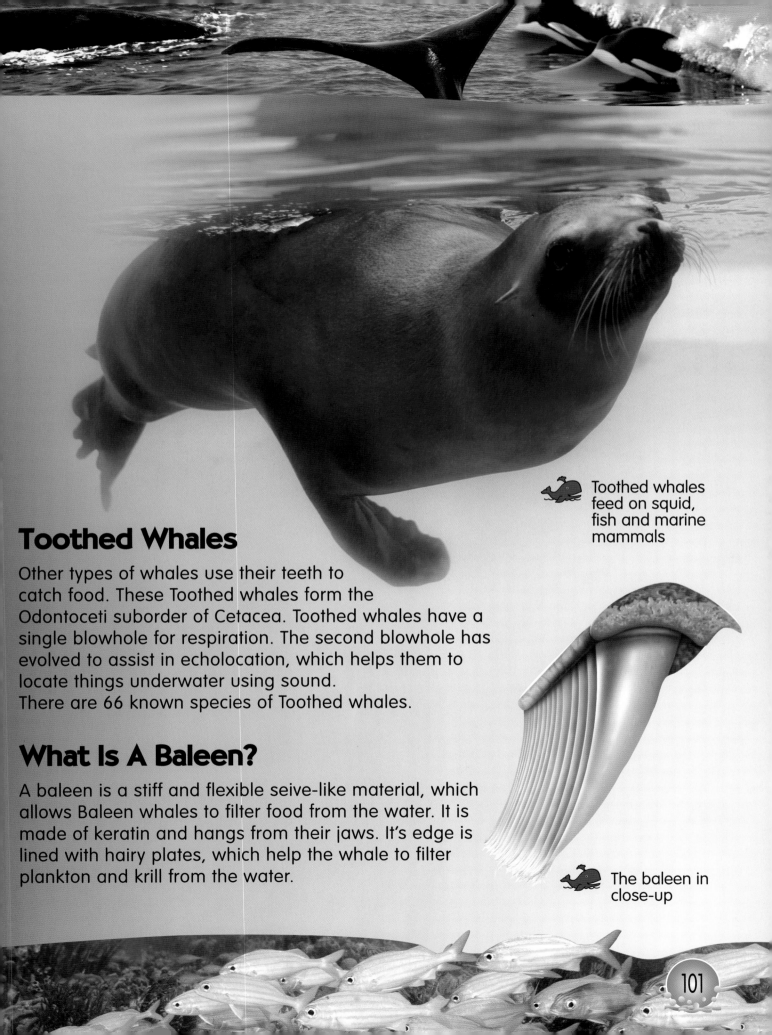

Toothed Whales

Other types of whales use their teeth to
catch food. These Toothed whales form the
Odontoceti suborder of Cetacea. Toothed whales have a
single blowhole for respiration. The second blowhole has
evolved to assist in echolocation, which helps them to
locate things underwater using sound.
There are 66 known species of Toothed whales.

Toothed whales
feed on squid,
fish and marine
mammals

What Is A Baleen?

A baleen is a stiff and flexible seive-like material, which
allows Baleen whales to filter food from the water. It is
made of keratin and hangs from their jaws. It's edge is
lined with hairy plates, which help the whale to filter
plankton and krill from the water.

The baleen in
close-up

The Baleen Family

The Mysticeti suborder of Baleen whales contains four families and fourteen species of whales.

What Are They?

Baleen whales are some of the largest animals on Earth. Not all Baleen whales feed in the same way. There are some that swim and gulp food. Others keep their mouths open at all times and food filters through. Some whales do both. Another technique of feeding is known as benthic feeding, which means they find their food in the silt of the sea bed.

 Humpback whales have white patches on their undersides

Baleen whales feed on different types of fish, krill and plankton

Fun Fact

Right whales may have as many as 100 tiny hairs on their upper jaws and around 300 on their lower jaws.

Humpback Whales

One of the most impressive Baleen whales is the Humpback. They are known for the beautiful and haunting songs they produce and their complex system of feeding. Humpback whales can dive for as long as 30 minutes. They get their name from the stance they take while diving. Most Humpback whales live for around 45-50 years.

I Am Right

Right whales have lower jaws that look like bows and very big heads. Little is known about them, but it is believed that they live for over 60 years. The people who traditionally hunted these creatures thought that they were the 'right', or correct, whales to hunt because of the amount of blubber they contained. This is where their name comes from.

Right whales are black or dark grey in colour with patches of either brown or white, or both

Toothy Smiles

Toothed whales form a suborder of Cetaceans called Odontoceti and are characterised by their teeth and the hunting of prey.

Toothed whales use their teeth to catch food such as squid, fish and marine mammals

Look At My Teeth

Toothed whales are different from Baleen whales mainly because they have teeth to catch their food. However, they cannot use their peg-shaped teeth to chew their food. Some species of Toothed whales have as many as 250 teeth, while others may only have two!

Sperm Whales

Sperm whales are the largest among all Toothed whales. They may grow to a length of around 17–20 m (50–60 ft) and weigh 36–45 tonnes (40–50 tons). They also have the largest head of all animals, which houses a very big brain that may weigh as much as 9 kg (20 lbs). Sperm whales are protected by a covering of spermaceti oil produced by an organ located in their head. They can live for more than 70 years.

 Sperm whales are the largest Toothed whales and cannot move very fast because of their huge bulk

Fun Fact

Sperm whales are often found logging. This is where they lie still on the surface with their tail hanging down.

Narwhals

Narwhals are fascinating Toothed whales, best known for the single long tooth that the males possess. These whales are found in the icy Arctic region, but are very rarely seen. As a result, very little is known about them, which adds to their mystery. Male narwhals have two teeth in their upper jaw. The left tooth grows long, and is usually twisted and hollow inside. They are probably meant for protection. Narwhals usually travel in pods of 4–20 whales, and feed mainly on shrimp, squid and small marine mammals.

 The single long tooth of a narwhal can grow to 3 m (10 ft) in length!

Feeling Blue

The largest and loudest animal on Earth
is the Blue whale.

We Are Big

Female Blue whales are usually larger in size
than males. On average they grow to a
length of 25 m (80 ft) and weigh about 109
tonnes (120 tons). The largest Blue whale ever
measured was 29 m (94 ft) in length and
weighed 158 tonnes (174 tons)! Blue whales
also have huge hearts that weigh around
450 kg (1,000 lbs).

 Blue whales are much larger
in size than any other creature
that lives underwater

How Do I Look?

Blue whales are huge Baleen whales that have
two blowholes and a thick layer of blubber. They
are usually blue-grey in colour and have grooves
in their throats which allow them to expand while
feeding. These huge whales have yellow, grey or
brown patches on their underbelly. Their dorsal
fins are small and sickle-shaped and found near
their tail. The Blue whale's blood alone weighs
6,400 kg (14,000 lbs).

 Blue whales have
flippers that measure
2.4 m (8 ft) in length and
7.6 m (25 ft) in width

What's Cooking?

Blue whales are carnivores that feed on small fish, plankton and tiny crustaceans such as krill with the help of their baleen plates. They are gulpers – that is, they take a gulp of water and then filter the water out, retaining any food it contained. Around 320 pairs of black baleen plates are present in their upper jaws that have dark grey bristles at the edge. Blue whales also have huge tongues, which weigh a staggering 3.8 tonnes (4 tons)! A Blue whale of average size may eat up to 4,100 kg (9,000 lbs) of food daily. That is a lot of food!

Blue whales feed on large amounts of krill, plankton, other tiny crustaceans and small fish

Summer Holiday

Whales are known to migrate thousands of miles every year to feed and give birth to their calves.

Whales carry out seasonal migrations every year. They usually travel together

Time To Go

Whales, like most Cetaceans, follow seasonal migration. Baleen whales are known for their particularly long migration routes. Most whales travel in small groups or pods and move to cold-water areas for feeding and warm-water regions for giving birth to their young.

Fun Fact

Adult Humpback whales do not feed during the winter months. Instead, they live off their layer of fat, called blubber.

A Long Long Way

The longest migration route of any whale is undertaken by the Grey whale. They cover a huge distance of 19,312 km (12,000 miles) in a single trip, to and from their destination. In October they start migrating from the feeding grounds at the Chukchi and Bering seas, southwards to their calving grounds in Baja California, Mexico. They remain there for another 2-3 months, after which they return to their feeding grounds.

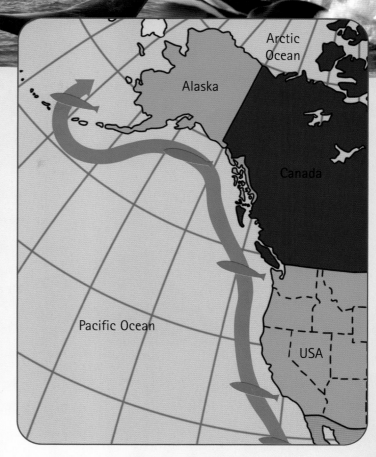

 Grey whales carry out the longest migrations among all whales. The migration takes several months

Humpback Migration

Humpback whales also travel a long distance during their seasonal migration, covering about 6,437 km (4,000 miles) each way. They give birth to their calves in warm tropical waters during the winter months and then migrate to the cold Polar regions to feed during summer. These whales usually do not take much rest during their long journeys. They are also capable of swimming quite quickly, reaching speeds of about 14 km/h (9 mph) at times.

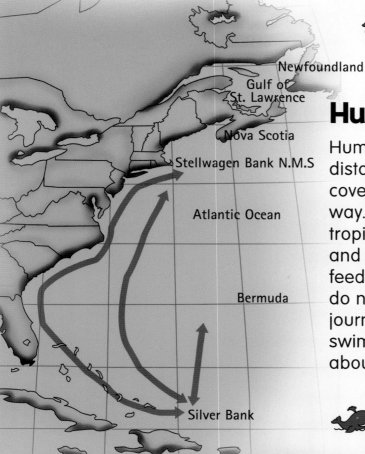

 Humpback whales migrate along the eastern coast of North America

In Books and Culture

Numerous references are made to whales in both classical and popular literature. They are also associated with divinity in many cultures.

Holy References

References to whales are found in the Holy Bible. The King James version of the Holy Bible speaks about whales in four different places. In the book of Genesis, it mentions how God created the great whales. The Prophet Jonah was said to have been swallowed by a whale. This reference is also made in the Qur'an, the central religious text of Islam.

The Holy Bible has as many as four references to whales

The Sea of Marmara

Divine Whales

In parts of Vietnam and Ghana, whales are considered holy. They have been known to hold funerals for dead whales found on the beach - a custom that has been inherited from Vietnam's early sea-based Austro-Asiatic culture. Whales are celebrated through songs, art and whale watching in many parts of the world, such as Kodiak Alaska and Sitka.

 Vietnamese fishermen sometimes hold funerals for dead whales

In Literature

Whales have been mentioned in literature many times. The Old English poem *Beowulf* describes the sea as a 'whale-road'. Procopius of Caesarea, an important Eastern Roman scholar, spoke about a whale who destroyed fisheries in the Sea of Marmara. Then, of course, there is the American novel *Moby-Dick,* about a whaling boat's seach for a Sperm whale.

Fun Fact

The word 'whale' is no longer used in the New International Version of the Christian Bible.

No Longer Around

Whales evolved over millions of years, from land-living creatures the size of modern wolves, to water-living mammals that breathe through their blowholes.

Pakicetus

One of the earliest ancestors of modern day whales was the Pakicetus. These now extinct creatures, roamed the Earth during the early Eocene period, millions of years ago. Their fossils have been found in Pakistan, hence their name, in an area that was once a part of the ancient Tethys Sea coastline. These early 'whales' were completely land-living, about the same size as wolves, and looked very much like another now extinct creature, called the Mesonychid.

Ambulocetus

The Ambulocetus or 'walking whales' were some of the earliest whales that roamed the Earth. These ancient creatures could move on land as well as in water, and their fossils are very important in the study of whale evolution from land-living mammals to water-living ones. Their teeth show that they could survive in both fresh and salt waters.

 Skeletons of the Pakicetus were first discovered in 2001 in Pakistan

The Ambulocetus had a specially designed nose that allowed it to swallow whilst underwater

Fun Fact

Some Cryptozoologists believe that the Basilosaurus, or an evolved version of it, still exists as some form of sea serpent.

Basilosaurus

The Basilosaurus was a fascinating ancestor of whales that had a giant snake-like long body. It was a completely water-living creature and did not have the ability to move on land. Found around 35–40 million years ago, the Basilosaurus measured about 18 m (60 ft) in length. Their fossils show tiny remnants of hind limbs and they also had small flukes.

The Basilosaurus

In Danger

The greatest threat to whales comes from us – humans!
Activities such as whaling have greatly depleted their numbers.

Hunted

For centuries whales have been hunted for their meat, baleen plates, blubber and oil. This activity is known as whaling and was extensively practised during the 19th and 20th centuries greatly reducing the number of whales. As a result, whaling has now been banned in several countries to protect their numbers. However, some countries, such as Japan, Iceland and Norway, still allow whaling, despite international condemnation.

Fun Fact

Toxic chemicals have been found to cause loss of hearing in whales.

Many whale deaths are caused by accident as bycatch, where they become trapped in trawler nets

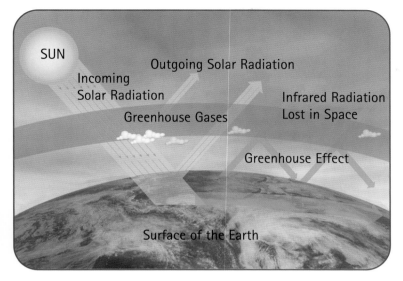

SUN

Incoming
Solar Radiation

Outgoing Solar Radiation

Infrared Radiation
Lost in Space

Greenhouse Gases

Greenhouse Effect

Surface of the Earth

 Global warming is raising the temperature of the world and affecting the conditions that are necessary for the survival of whales

The Environment

Environmental issues, such as global warming and climate change, are affecting whale numbers. The warming of the waters is killing krill, which is the main source of food for many whales. Moreover, Seismic testing, which is used to find gas and oil, is very harmful as it affects the hearing and echolocation abilities of whales.

The Human Factor

Harmful human practises cause the greatest damage to whale populations around the world. Dumping of dangerous toxins in and around the waters where whales live is destroying their habitats. Careless fishing and accidents with ships are also responsible for their depleting numbers.

 Litter pollutes the seas and is washed up on our beaches

Facts at a Glance

🐋 Blue whales are the largest animals in the world. They can grow to a length equivalent to the height of a 9-storey building!

🐋 Dwarf Sperm whales are the smallest whales. Adults measure around 2.6 m (8.5 ft) in length.

🐋 Shortfin Pilot whales are the fastest swimming whales. They can reach a speed of 48 km/h (30 mph).

🐋 Grey whales migrate the longest distance, covering about 1,9312 km (12,000 miles) every year.

🐋 The largest brain in the animal world belongs to the Sperm whale.

🐋 When Right whales die their bodies float on the surface.

Humpback whales are sometimes called 'singing' whales.

Fin whales use their flukes as weapons when defending themselves.

The most endangered whale in the ocean is the Northern Right whale.

Right whales have the longest baleen among all whales.

Right whales also make the lowest frequency sound of any whale, at 3–5 Hz.

Whales and hippos are closely related.

It is believed that narwhals gave rise to the legend of the unicorns.

In each mouthful, a Blue whales takes in equal to around 256,000 glasses of water, which is then expelled through the baleen plates.

Several toothed whales use sonar to locate their prey.

Glossary

Agonistic: Eager to fight; agitated; aggressive.

Anatomy: The structure of the body of an animal or plant, or any of its parts.

Auditory bulla: A hollow bone that covers and protects the middle and inner ear.

Axis: A line around which a rotating body spins.

Barbel: Thin, whisker-like organs found near the mouth of certain fish and sharks.

Bask: To lie in warmth or soak up the sun.

Biologist: A scientist or an expert who studies living organisms.

Camouflage: The ability to merge with the surroundings so that an animal is not easily distinguished from the things around it.

Cartilage: A tough, elastic tissue found in the ears and nose.

Circulatory system: A system in the body of an animal which regulates the flow of blood to and from the cells, and transports nutrients, gases and water throughout the body.

Coastline: The boundary of a sea shore, or coast.

Contamination: To make a substance impure by mixing it with dangerous and harmful substances.

Contract: To reduce in size; shrink.

Crustaceans: Any of the creatures, such as crabs, lobsters and shrimps, which belong to the class Crustacea.

Cryptozoologist: A group of people who look for proof of the existence of creatures that are rumoured to exist, such as the Loch Ness monster.

Evolution: The gradual change in an organism to adapt itself to its environment.

Expand: To increase in size.

Fossil: Any part or impression of the body of an animal or plant that existed a long time ago, such as footprints or the skeleton.

Fusiform: Refers to a body which is narrow or tapering   at its two ends.

Gills: The organ that fish use to breathe.

Global warming: The increase in the average temperature of the air near the Earth's surface, particularly in recent years.

Hierarchy: A system of ranking people or things according to their importance.

Illegal: Against the law.

Inaudible: Any sound that cannot be heard.

Infant mortality: The rate of death among the young ones of a species.

Insulation: The prevention of loss of heat, sound or electricity into the surrounding area.

Jaws: The bones inside the mouth in which teeth are fixed.

Lagoon: A shallow lake which is cut off from the sea by coral reefs or sand bars.

Larynx: An organ in animals in which the vocal cords and other vocal organs lie.

Liver: A reddish-brown organ in animals that plays an important role in digestion.

Mammal: Warm-blooded animals that share common features, such as giving birth to live young and nursing them.

Membrane: A thin fibrous tissue that covers or lines cells and organs in animals and plants.

Molar: A tooth that grinds food.

Mollusc: Invertebrates, such as snails, slugs, octopuses, squids, clams and mussels.

Mottled: Blotches or spots in the colouring of a body.

Mythology: A set of stories arising out of traditions and beliefs.

Navigate: To move or find one's way.

Nictitating membrane: A thin fold of skin under the eyelids that can be used to cover the eyes. It is usually found in reptiles, birds and certain mammals.

Notch: A V-shaped cut.

Olfactory nerve: The nerves that are responsible for the sense of smell.

Opportunistic hunters: Hunters who take the best advantage of the conditions available to them for hunting.

Plankton: Tiny plants and animals that are found floating on the surface of seas and lakes.

Predator: An animal that hunts other animals for food.

Predatory: The tendency or characteristic of an animal to hunt other animals for food.

Radiate: To send out, or emit.

Remora: A long, flat fish with spiny fins found in the ocean. It attaches itself to other fish and rocks underwater with the help of sucking discs on the top of its head.

Requiem shark: Any shark belonging to the Carcharhinidae family. This includes the tiger shark and the lemon shark.

Scavenger: An animal or bird that feeds on already dead or decaying matter.

Streamline: Designed in such a way as to offer the least possible resistance to either air or water.

Temperate: Moderate or mild in temperature. Not too cold or too hot.

Tendrils: Long thread-like structures.

Tissue: A group of cells in the body of an animal or plant that comprise its make-up.

Torpedo: A cigar-shaped under water missile that is usually launched from a submarine, a craft or ship.

Toxin: A poisonous substance usually produced by living organisms.

Ultrasound: Sound which trave at a very high frequency. Hum beings usually cannot hear it.

Vibrate: Continuous and rapid movement to and fro.

Index

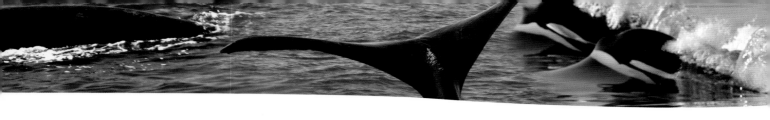